Nicholas Thomas
obtained a doctorate in 1986
on the history and culture of the Marquesas Islands at
the Australian National University in Canberra, where
he is now a Senior Research Fellow. He has conducted
extensive fieldwork on the cultures of the Pacific and
is currently researching contemporary art and the
politics of identity in New Zealand.

WORLD OF ART

This famous series
provides the widest available
range of illustrated books on art in all its aspects.
If you would like to receive a complete list
of titles in print please write to:
THAMES AND HUDSON
30 Bloomsbury Street, London WC1B 3QP
In the United States please write to:
THAMES AND HUDSON INC.
500 Fifth Avenue, New York, New York 10110

Printed in Singapore

Nicholas Thomas

Oceanic Art

182 illustrations, 26 in color

Thames and Hudson

For Anna Jolly

Frontispiece: Korawai man with a shield in a tree house, Tajan village, Irian Jaya, 1979. Photo Tobias Schneebaum.

First published in the United States of America in 1995 by Thames and Hudson Inc., 500 Fifth Avenue New York, New York, 10110

Library of Congress Catalog Card Number 94-61059 ISBN 0-500-20281-8

Printed and bound in Singapore

Contents

1 Map of the Pacific Islands.

MEXICO

Tropic of Cancer

HAWAII

P O L Y N E S I A

Equator

MARQUESAS

TUAMOTU ARCHIPELAGO

COOK ISLANDS

Huahine
Borabora
Tahiti
Raiatea
SOCIETY ISLANDS

AUSTRAL ISLANDS

Mangareva

Tropic of Capricorn

Easter Island
(Rapanui)

PACIFIC OCEAN

2 Baining mask, New Britain, collected *c*.1900. Ht 29⅞ in.

Introduction

To look at Oceanic art is to look at remarkable things. Some, such as masks, canoes and carved or painted houses, are awesome or disconcerting; others, such as polished stone personal ornaments and the designs of barkcloth and woven mats, are beautiful and intricate. But to look *at* is not the same as to look *into*. If Pacific art forms are indeed striking on the surface, what is behind the surface may be still more challenging and provoking. Looking into art forms means examining their parts and composition, as well as the effect of the whole.

Looking beyond surfaces also means looking into contexts. Oceanic art was and is created in cultural milieux that do not share Western premises about what art is, how it is produced, or what its effects are. A carving that has human characteristics is not necessarily a 'representation' of a human being or an ancestor. It may be better understood as an embodiment of that ancestor, as one expression of that ancestor, or it may be a physical container that an ancestor or spirit can be induced to inhabit at certain times. On the other hand, designs that appear to be abstract to an outsider may denote specific animals or mythological figures for local viewers. Insiders are likely to share assumptions about the general character and effect of art forms, but some will be more knowledgeable than others about the figures represented, and about the meanings of particular motifs. In some cases there may be an elaborate indigenous discourse about artifacts and designs, but things are more often simply produced and taken to stand for themselves – as visual effects that require no commentary or verbal elucidation. If accounts of the meanings of paintings and carvings are elaborated at all, they may be secret and restricted ideally, if not in practice, to persons who are members of a particular cult, to elders or initiated men. This secrecy or obscurity will sometimes be precisely what makes the object powerful – what is hidden being less important than the fact that it is concealed.

Oceanic art thus challenges a whole range of Western expectations concerning knowledge and social relationships as well as art. While the elements that distinguish this culture need to be understood, it is

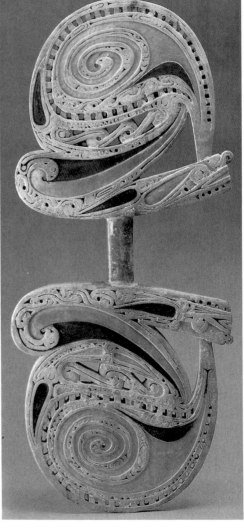

3 (*above*) Door, Ouébia, north New Caledonia, collected 1911. Ht 65 in.

4 (*right*) Dance paddle, Kilivila, Trobriand Islands, collected 1885. Ht 30½ in.

5 Sacred men's house, Sarmi, north-west New Guinea. Ht 30 ft.

important that they are not reduced to the merely exotic. Although rituals and genealogies often create intimate bonds between people and their land, as exchange relations between people and deities ensure life, abundance and well-being, Pacific cultures are not pervaded by harmony and spiritual interconnectedness with the environment, as a superficial New Age image of tribal societies might suggest. What is different is both exaggerated and diminished by stereotypic ideas about mystical, ancestral cults or 'primitive mentalities'. The idea that life is governed by a spirit world at once understates the significance of what is mundane and practical, and also obscures more important cultural differences that permeate artistic production.

The meanings and effects of Oceanic art are not wholly alien to those of other artistic systems, in part because there seem to be psychological universals that influence art everywhere. Some colours and patterns are reproduced and elaborated upon because they dazzle and disconcert; symmetry, shapes like eyes and combinations of red, black and white all have certain effects upon human vision and cognition. The intention behind an image, however, can only have a local motivation and context. At a social, rather than a perceptual or cognitive level, there are other universals that enter into virtually all art traditions: the fact of death, the relationship with the dead that a community seeks to sustain or erase, and the problem of creating continuity out of contingency and impermanence, are issues negotiated everywhere, but understood in particular and different terms in the Pacific.

Europeans and islanders are joined as well as separated by histories. Relations of exchange, conflict and mutual influence between Pacific peoples, Europeans, Americans and others have had profound and diverse ramifications for Pacific art forms since the eighteenth century. Just as ethnographic artifacts were depicted by the artists of exploratory voyages, and as Oceanic forms inspired Gauguin and many others subsequently, indigenous artists responded to contact with Europeans by depicting introduced things, and by using introduced materials and styles. In some cases, the changes that took place are best understood as substitutions. Finely woven mats with red feather borders might now incorporate wool; the motifs typically carved on clubs would be applied also to new weapons such as muskets; in the same way, exchange systems that previously circulated shell valuables and pork now circulate tinned food, beer and cash.

In other cases, adopted techniques have had effects that are at once deeper and less obvious. A carving might appear distinctive and traditional, yet be produced with an iron rather than a stone tool, which is conducive to a more intricate treatment of the same motifs and possibly signals a different attitude towards the final product. Illustrations in missionary books or other Western publications might prompt a figurative or narrative treatment of themes that had previously been handled far more allusively. In the first case, the outsider might assume that a piece was traditional because it appeared broadly consistent with traditional carving; in the second, he or she might assume that the maker was completely divorced from traditional culture. Not only would both assumptions be wrong for the particular works, they would also impose the wrong expectations in general.

'Traditional' art was always evolving and could change rapidly and drastically if a new cult arose with distinct iconography and paraphernalia, or if exchange relations with other groups created new contacts or introduced new materials. A piece made just before European contact expresses a particular moment in a process of cultural and

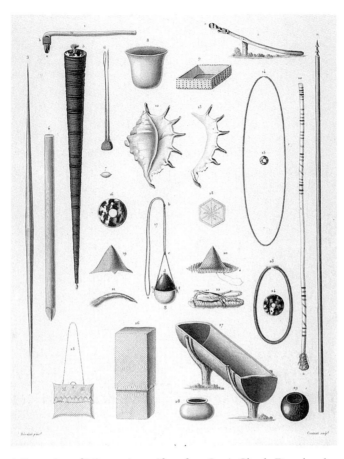

6 Engraving of Micronesian artifacts from Louis Claude Desaulses de Freycinet, *Voyage autour du monde*, 1824–6.

stylistic development, but has no greater status than one made a hundred years later or earlier. On the other hand, changes in style and motifs, and even the overall adoption of European techniques of oil painting and printmaking, do not signify a lack of continuity with tradition. Even if discontinuity is conspicuous in meanings as well as techniques and styles, the art forms are not appropriately understood as 'assimilated', because the content and perspectives of work remain typically grounded in indigenous experiences and histories.

13

7 Prehistoric figure, Enga,
western Highlands, Papua New
Guinea. Ht 7¾ in.

PACIFIC CULTURES AND HISTORIES

The more remote archipelagoes in the central and eastern Pacific have a short prehistory in global terms. The ancestors of the Hawaiians, Easter Islanders and Maori formed a single population in central Polynesia before the marginal islands were settled between AD 400 and 900; the differences between the art styles produced on those islands at the time of European contact thus arose quite late in the course of relatively short separate histories.

The prehistory of the Pacific as a whole is more complex. A distinction needs to be made between the island of New Guinea (now divided between the independent nation of Papua New Guinea and West Papua, or Irian Jaya, which is part of Indonesia) and the rest of Oceania. Most of New Guinea is occupied by speakers of Papuan languages and has been inhabited for more than forty thousand years; this early phase of settlement extended into neighbouring islands to the north and east, including parts of the Solomons. Most of the other Pacific archipelagoes, on the other hand, were settled much later by speakers of Austronesian languages who moved into the region from insular south-east Asia between four thousand and three thousand years ago. Although these people must originally have been quite distinct from the earlier settlers, there is now no clear cultural boundary that corresponds with the basic linguistic division, but rather a plethora of regional differences. Particular areas, such as the Sepik basin, the Papuan gulf and the Highlands, tend to be broadly distinct in social and cultural terms, and are oriented towards particular forms and styles of artistic expression. However, the patterns of variation are complicated by trade and interaction, and by the expansion and migration of certain populations. These shifts proceeded before European contact, but were often subsequently accelerated or reoriented by a host of factors, including the introduction of guns and diseases, changing exchange relations and the expansion of Christian missions.

The Austronesian expansion into the Pacific is associated by archaeologists with a distinctive pottery style known as Lapita. The earliest **8** fragments have been found in the New Britain–Admiralty Islands area, but Lapita is spread right across the south-western Pacific from coastal New Guinea to Fiji and western Polynesia, suggesting that one population with a distinctive culture settled in the region relatively rapidly. Lapita sites imply a primary orientation towards fishing and trade, complemented by horticulture and the domestication of pigs, dogs and chickens, and linguistic analysis suggests social differentiation of rank on the basis of elder and younger. Though evidence with any direct bearing on culture and art is limited, many Lapita fragments bear

8 Reconstruction of Lapita pot design, from fragments from the Nessadiou site, New Caledonia.

incised curvilinear motifs and some faces and human forms that broadly resemble later barkcloth and tattooing designs.

The area including Fiji and western Polynesia was settled about three thousand years ago, and at this point there appears to have been an interval of perhaps a thousand years before further settlement took place to the east, during which time a distinctively Polynesian culture developed, which differed from those evolving separately in New Caledonia, Vanuatu, the Solomons and islands further west. In eastern Polynesia, the Marquesas and the Society Islands appear to have been settled first, and the more remote fringes, including New Zealand, much later. Micronesia was settled from both west and east between three thousand and two thousand years ago and reflects a convergence of Oceanic and insular south-east Asian influences.

In the western Pacific, and particularly on larger islands in the Solomons and Vanuatu, coastal areas were no doubt occupied initially, but growing populations moved gradually into the often mountainous interiors. Distinct lifestyles based in different environments emerged, which were later marked by indigenous ethnic distinctions between 'bush' and 'saltwater' people. As populations became denser, social differentiation also proceeded, with the result that ritual activities, craft specialization, mythology and art forms became extraordinarily diversified within small areas. It is difficult to avoid the inference that diversification somehow became a social objective in itself, as though populations elaborated the distinctiveness of their own art forms, practices and languages in order to define themselves more clearly against their neighbours. At the same time, however, artifacts and ritual knowledge were frequently bartered and generalized similarities between art objects across certain regions attest to the spread of motifs and styles, which no doubt often acquired new and different meanings as they moved from one society to another. Mutual influences and appropriations thus entered into a larger cultural dynamic through which selves and others were identified.

Although brief meetings between islanders and Europeans took place from the sixteenth century onwards, sustained interaction began only in the second half of the eighteenth century. Explorers encountered, and were encountered by, the people of Tahiti, Hawaii, Tonga, New Zealand and many smaller islands in Polynesia; although parts of Vanuatu and New Caledonia were also visited by Bougainville and Cook, intrusions in the western Pacific were generally more limited until much later. In Polynesia and Micronesia it was not long before frequent visits were made by whalers and traders seeking provisions,

9 Prehistoric petroglyph,
Tipaerui Valley, Tahiti.

water, sexual contacts and local resources such as tortoiseshell and
sandalwood. From the end of the eighteenth century, also, the London
Missionary Society was active, unsuccessfully in Tonga and the   12
Marquesas, but to greater effect in Tahiti, which subsequently became
a base for evangelism westwards into the Cook Islands, Samoa and
elsewhere; before the mid-nineteenth century, other Protestant
denominations and Catholic orders followed, seeking to carve up the   14
region and compete for adherents.

These casual and more sustained relations had diverse ramifications:
iron tools, cloth and guns were introduced, access to European trade
articles became a new source of power and prestige for warrior-chiefs,
and islanders themselves travelled on ships and encountered other
Pacific peoples and their artifacts. Even on the Cook voyages, barkcloth obtained through barter in Easter Island and Tonga was taken to
Tahiti and New Zealand; other artifacts obtained at one island were
exchanged away at another, and many islanders would have at least
seen the specimens of other islanders' art that officers, natural histori-
ans and sailors were avidly collecting. The early voyages, therefore, not

17

only inaugurated relations of exchange and mutual influence between Europeans and Oceanic people, they also provided opportunities for new or intensified contacts among Pacific islanders themselves.

The voyages also marked the first phase of intensive European collecting of Oceanic art: objects obtained on British, Russian, French and American voyages that have passed through dealers' hands, private collections, and sometimes several museums, are now dispersed in institutions all over the world, more often than not without satisfying documentation. White visitors were so eager to acquire certain items that it is likely that the production of a kind of early 'tourist art' began in the 1770s or very soon afterwards. Pieces were sold more regularly and systematically in a few areas from the late nineteenth century onwards, and in many others only recently. The quality and appearance of work did not necessarily change rapidly, but over time, European interests have had both obvious and subtle ramifications in work produced for local use as well as that intended for barter or sale.

Traders introduced new tools and Western goods, but also often made new supplies of raw materials or indigenous valuables available. The nineteenth-century traders from New England who were seeking sandalwood and bêche-de-mer (both for Chinese markets) in Fiji realized that Fijians valued sperm whale teeth more highly than other trade goods such as beads, iron or cloth, and imported great quantities of ivory in this and other forms. Although whale teeth were presumably already used to a limited extent in ceremonial exchange in Fiji, the number in circulation expanded dramatically over the early to mid-nineteenth century. Necklaces and breastplates made from sawn ivory pieces were produced in much greater numbers and no

10 Rapanui boy selling wooden figures, c. 1930.

11 Breastplate, Fiji, owned and worn by the paramount chief,
Tanoa, *c.*1840. W. 10⅝ in.

longer restricted to men of the highest rank. In the 1930s, the plane-
loads of pearlshell, flown into the Papua New Guinea Highlands by
prospectors to pay for labour, had a similar impact on the circulation
and form of shell breastplates, which were and are among the most
important items of male decoration.

The effect of Christianity was both positive and negative. In many
areas, missionaries encouraged the destruction of cult objects that they
took to be 'idols' and generally worked towards the abandonment of
indigenous religion, with which much art was associated. Many individual artifacts were also mutilated in order to remove conspicuous
genitalia; consequently, tattooing – done in part to enhance a person's
sexual attractiveness – was sometimes regarded as a mark of heathen
licentiousness and discouraged for such reasons. On the other hand,
the missionary attitude towards apparently abstract or decorative art
was frequently positive, since pottery and the manufacture of ornaments attested to a commendable propensity for industry; women's
products, such as mats, barkcloth and baskets, were tolerated, if not

12 George Baxter, *The Reception of the Reverend John Williams at Tanna in the South Seas*, 1843. 8⅜ × 12½ in.

13 Priest's dish, Fiji, early nineteenth century. L. 18¼ in. The priest would drink a strong infusion of kava (the indigenous narcotic) through a wooden straw, to induce possession by the spirit. Associations between shamanic inspiration and birds were widely noted in Oceania.

fostered. Some missions also encouraged the elaboration of indigenous sculpture and painting with Christian themes in place of pagan ones; such pieces were often incorporated in churches that might themselves share either the external form or internal arrangement of indigenous architecture.

Conversion to Christianity was often marked by the adoption of European clothing, and women converts were frequently enrolled in sewing classes organized by wives of missionaries. Local garments, such as grass skirts, were on the whole abandoned, but new cloth products, including elaborate quilts in central and eastern Polynesia, acquired some of the cultural significance of barkcloth and pandanus mats, despite the dissimilarity of the material and decorative styles. In the western Pacific, many missionaries were not Europeans, but Polynesian teachers, who frequently introduced techniques of mat-making and weaving from their own home communities. While Melanesian art traditions and those of western Polynesia were distantly related in prehistory, the residual similarities that must always have

20

14 The Roman Catholic Church, Ariseli, Torricelli Mountains, north-west of Maprik, East Sepik, Papua New Guinea, 1971. The triangular, painted facade is closely adapted from that of an Abelam ceremonial house.

been obvious at the basic level of weaving techniques have been overlain and reinforced by more recent contacts and borrowings. Objects such as the pandanus basket or mat have therefore become both bearers of particular local styles and, in their overall form, markers of a larger Melanesian or Pacific identity.

Most Oceanic peoples have dealt with some period of formal colonial rule, which in several cases persists into the present. French Polynesia, including the Society Islands, the Marquesas, the Austral Islands and the Tuamotu archipelago, came under French control in the 1840s, as did New Caledonia in 1853; in both cases there is now a degree of local autonomy within firm French metropolitan control. The Cook Islands and Niue retain strong links with New Zealand; American Samoa and Guam are still formally part of the United States, and most of the rest of Micronesia has only a limited degree of independence within a 'compact of free association' with the USA. The New Hebrides (now Vanuatu) was under a joint Anglo-French administration from 1907 until independence in 1980; Fiji and the

Solomon Islands were British colonies from the late nineteenth century until, respectively, 1970 and 1978; Papua New Guinea experienced German, British and Australian rule as well as partial Japanese occupation during the Second World War before independence in 1975. Other peoples, such as the Hawaiians and Maori have become minorities within settler societies, and continue to fight for cultural and political autonomy; the West Papuans are in a similar situation within Indonesia.

The colonial powers were often indifferent to indigenous societies rather than actively interventionist; in many cases missions introduced education and medical services before official systems were established. Indigenous warfare and cult activities that were taken to be disorderly or threatening were suppressed, and this process of 'pacification' sometimes led to the destruction or abandonment of art forms associated with head-hunting, such as war canoes and skull shrines. In other cases, demand on the part of collectors and tourists kept the production of canoes, shields and weapons alive after fighting itself had ceased. The foreign intrusions that have often concerned Pacific islanders most, especially in recent years, stem not from formal colonial rule, but from commercial activities – mining, logging and Japanese driftnet fishing – which are exhausting natural resources. Protest against such overexploitation and against nuclear testing at Mururoa and in Micronesia figures in much contemporary Pacific art, uniting islanders of diverse backgrounds and appealing to non-islanders with environmentalist and pacifist concerns.

In some regions, local societies were irrevocably transformed and people became peasant producers marginal to larger societies or wage-labourers on plantations, in tourist enterprises, mining or forestry. Elsewhere, as in the New Guinea Highlands, contact and colonization arrived late and retreated early; although Highlands societies have certainly changed dramatically as a result of pacification, Christianity, mining and coffee-growing, these developments, rather than overwhelming it, have been conspicuously absorbed into a developing indigenous system. Imported goods and cash are integrated with competitive ceremonial exchange, which proceeds with as much vigour as renewed clan warfare. In this context, what is conspicuous is not the disappearance of indigenous art, which was predicted by colonists who assumed that Pacific peoples and cultures would 'die out' in the face of European expansion, but the rapid elaboration of traditional forms through the incorporation of new motifs and media. In other regions, such as many parts of eastern Polynesia, traditional knowledge did

15 Bride price banner, Wahgi people, Papua New Guinea Highlands, 1980. Cash exchanged for a bride is displayed in the same way that shells would traditionally have been presented.

largely fail to survive the depopulation that occurred, which in some cases reduced indigenous populations by more than ninety per cent. Despite the consequent social fragmentation, a sense of indigenous distinctiveness has been sustained, and there is now an interest in re-creating local art forms, often in the context of neo-traditional craft production for tourists.

In late phases of colonial rule, as British and Australian authorities sought to encourage self-government, the preservation and mainte-nance of traditional culture received more systematic official patron-age in Papua New Guinea, the Solomons and Vanuatu. Regional and national cultural centres were established; the revival of arts that had been abandoned was promoted; and some institutions and buildings associated with the independent states sought an indigenous architec-tural idiom or drew upon traditional motifs. Cultural revival, however, took place in many areas quite independently of official support, and

23

is often politically opposed to central governments or continuing colonial control. Traditional art forms, which in many cases are sacred and secret, still relate uneasily to Christianity and commercialization. In some areas, artifacts for tourists, to which local people attach little worth, are clearly differentiated from valuables possessing religious significance, while in other areas there may be acrimonious debate about the sale of traditional pieces to museums or collectors.

Across Oceania, therefore, the spectrum of contemporary artistic production embraces much continuity and novelty, and a variety of relations between local producers and consumers, and external markets. In some areas, work which follows directly from traditional art is produced primarily for local use in ceremonial or ritual contexts. Elsewhere, material closely related to traditional forms is produced partly for traditional reasons and partly for sale. In other cases, abandoned forms have been revived for collectors and tourists; in many areas new art forms have arisen, drawing upon both indigenous and Western influences and materials, and figuring in ceremonial exchange, community architecture and Christian ritual. Alongside art in rural areas, which is still closely connected with marriage, initiation and mortuary ritual, are primarily urban developments associated with nationalism and the politicized affirmation of indigenous ethnicity

24

16 (*opposite*) Men lined up behind a canoe displaying the shields they have for sale, Otsjanep village on the Ewta River, Casuarina Coast, south-west New Guinea, 1971.

17 (*right*) Shields used in contemporary fighting in the Papua New Guinea Highlands sometimes draw on commercial imagery. Kaipel Ka displays the shield he has decorated with a logo for South Pacific beer, 1990.

18 (*below*) Local bus, Papua New Guinea Highlands, 1990. Buses are a crucial link, not least for marriage purposes, between different groups in the Highlands.

(although village art forms may be equally politicized in ways that are less obvious to outsiders). Urban art frequently differs from traditional styles in the sense that industrial paints, fabrics and other materials are employed, but cultural continuities are nevertheless often manifest in approaches to form and subject matter. It ranges from officially sponsored expressions – most evident in government architecture – to popular painting and craft that typically integrate commercial iconography and the detritus of consumerism with an ebullient indigenous aesthetic.

19 Funerary effigy with tusks, south Malekula, Vanuatu, collected 1912. Ht 25¼ in.

ISSUES OF INTERPRETATION

The Oceanic art of the last two hundred years is diverse, as are the contexts within which work is currently produced – ranging from art schools in Port Moresby and Auckland to villages in the Highlands and the remotest eastern Polynesian atolls. It might follow that the problems that arise in interpreting Pacific art forms are similarly diverse, but some issues are in fact relevant to many contexts.

The point that there is no indigenous category corresponding with 'art' in the Western sense is often made, but in most areas, and especially in Polynesia, the products of specialists (known as *tohunga*, *tuhuna*, or a related term) were always considered special and valuable, because of the divine efficacy that their production both required and attested to. The category of 'art' may therefore be problematic, not so much because it marks off a domain of intensified aesthetic power and value, but because of the way in which the domain is defined. For the Western viewer, 'Oceanic art' is associated above all with objects in

26

museums, and although much indigenous energy indeed went into the carving, weaving and painting of material things, this conception is far too narrow.

It excludes ephemeral art such as sand drawings, body paintings and other forms of self-decoration. It presumes that artists produce objects such as masks, when in fact indigenous aesthetics may focus upon the order of gardens, the spatial arrangement of villages or dance grounds, or the moment of transmission of a gift. Throughout the Pacific, the human body is a locus of artistic elaboration; so too are animals such as the pig, notably in northern Vanuatu. In Malekula, where identifications between men and their pigs were and are especially deep, an extraordinary degree of energy went into the cultivation of boars' tusks. Knocking out the upper incisor permitted the lower to grow through a curve and eventually one, and sometimes two or three, full circles. Such a boar would become incapable of foraging for itself and would need to be hand-fed, but was understood to accumulate male soul-substance that would in turn be acquired by the male sacrificer at the moment when the boar was killed. Such sacrifices enabled men to acquire sanctity, titles and emblems of rank, and to move up through a hierarchy of grades, each associated with an exclusive sacred cooking-fire in the male club-house; the so-called 'graded society' was

19

20 Dancers during a pig festival in Papua New Guinea, 1979. Pigs are raised by women but transacted by men in New Guinea Highlands exchange ceremonies.

21 Ceremonial arrival of canoes, Gogodala, Papuan Gulf, 1975. In the early to mid-twentieth century, canoe races among the Gogodala people celebrated truces between warring clans. In the 1970s they came to mark anniversaries and celebrations, such as New Year's Day, Christmas and Independence Day.

fundamental to relationships of status and political authority in the area. The close identification between the pig and the man was such that boars' tusks were incorporated into the modelled heads of their owners or sacrificers, which were also painted with pig motifs. Elsewhere, on Ambae, the most highly valued pigs were selectively bred hermaphrodites, embodying a combination of male and female powers fundamental to cosmologies throughout the region, but rarely so explicitly realized. If art forms may be defined as modified or manipulated things that become aesthetic foci – in this region often, if not invariably, conveying sacredness and expressing political power

20

– these pigs certainly count as works of art to no less a degree than the slit gongs and masks that are so widely shown in museum collections.

It is also problematic if we presume that art inheres only in objects rather than in performances and practices. These may include casual, daily actions in which the motifs upon an implement or the tattoos on a person's body move; designs are not static, but mobile elements that enhance a sense of a body or an activity. But the routines of ordinary life in all Pacific societies were punctuated by more dramatic ceremonial occasions, such as initiations, canoe voyages to exchange valuables, 16,21 and competitive feasts; such occasions now also include commemora-

29

22 Two Mekeo men dressed for
a singing contest, Inawaia village,
Papua, 1921.

tions of national independence and moments in mission history.
Preparations for war, and indeed fighting itself, entailed elaborate
self-decoration and performance. All these occasions typically incorporated (as they still do) music, oratory, self-decoration and dance, as
well as paintings or carved artifacts that were (and are) often elements
of buildings or larger sacred precincts rather than isolated art forms.
While drums and slit gongs from Tahiti, Vanuatu and New Guinea are
frequently encountered in museum displays, and are indeed intricately
decorated, it is curiously easy to forget that they were not primarily
intended to be looked at, but were made to produce dance rhythms
and to heighten the pitch of ritual excitement. Shields, clubs and
spears were clearly produced for physical as well as aesthetic effect –
although the important point might be that their aesthetics engen-
dered fear and enhanced their impression of violence. On the other
hand, aesthetic effect sometimes is divorced from use: the formally
complex carving of Marquesan food bowls can be appreciated only

22,23
4
3,5
24

51

30

when those receptacles are not being used; at times other than feasts, they were probably hung up inside houses, much as paintings and other objects are displayed in domestic interiors elsewhere.

Political status and authority in Pacific societies was often defined by genealogical precedence, or by some other kind of acquired rank, but the most significant principle of differentiation was and is gender. In the everyday division of labour, the tasks of men and women are on the whole clearly distinguished and contrasted, and their juxtaposed capacities accounted for through myth. Women were frequently thought to contribute differently to the creation of the world and communities. They are often accorded an original creativity, which men somehow appropriated, and ritual frequently re-enacts this theft or eclipse of female power, appearing, perhaps, to parallel male appropriations of women's work in gardening and animal husbandry: the products are conspicuously deployed by men in ceremonial exchange and cult activities. Sexual inequality is easily misinterpreted,

23 (below) Man with dance shield, Buin district, Bougainville, Solomon Islands, 1912.

24 (below right) Slit gong, Atchin, East Malekula, Vanuatu. Ht 7 ft 2 in.

25 (*opposite*) *Malanggan* carving,
north New Ireland, collected 1895.
Ht 36⅝ in.

26 (*right*) Female figure, Nukuoro,
Caroline Islands, early nineteenth
century. Ht 15⅞ in.

27 (*far right*) Human figure, Rapanui.

however. With respect to the example of production, Marilyn
Strathern has pointed out that, 'As in a lunar eclipse, for the effects to
be registered, there can only be partial concealment and not oblitera-
tion' (*The Gender of the Gift*). The women's contribution that is
covered therefore remains distinctly marked, and it is precisely such
ambiguous covering that draws attention to what is beneath, and that
arguably often characterizes the layering of male and female powers
and domains in Pacific cultures and their art forms. Human sociality
itself may be understood as the product of a kind of male and female
'co-authorship' in which contributions are not equally displayed, but
nevertheless coexist.

Because gender is such a central metaphor, it operates in a complex
way: people are not necessarily unambiguously male or female, but
rather bearers of male and female attributes, to which attention is

drawn at appropriate moments in the life cycle in ritual and ceremonial exchange. Androgyny in the person may be expressed in art forms that incorporate both male and female symbolism – if not explicitly hermaphroditic features – as in the case of the Ambae pigs. This is to caution us: art forms such as clubs or barkcloth may seem to be unambiguously 'male' or 'female' objects, and they may indeed be largely produced and used more by one sex than the other, but their power may derive from a bisexual ambiguity. Female attributes may be combined with, or hidden within, a male form. Such meanings are not necessarily constant over time or place: display in one ceremonial context will draw attention to connotations that are at other times not so apparent.

27   It is frequently assumed that images of human beings in Oceanic art represent ancestors or gods, and are commemorated or worshipped as such. I have already noted that the principle of 'representation' may not be wholly apt; in the context of ceremonial performances especially, art may be more productively seen to create presences than to imitate or image something that exists elsewhere. Although some anthropomorphic sculptures, and others that are not recognizable as such, certainly do depict or represent gods or spirits, descriptions of this kind, often encountered on labels in museum displays, must be approached with scepticism. If a collector or dealer has little idea of the indigenous understanding and use of a piece, the impulse is often to assume that it represented a god or ancestor, and although curators might be expected to be more critical and scrupulous, there are many cases where the relevant ethnographic evidence is simply no longer available.

    Even if an ancestor is represented, the idea that the piece is commemorative may be wrong. The figure may in fact be produced specifically in order to be destroyed, as a way of marking the person's connections and persisting debts to other clans, which may be undone or finished, allowing kin to effect some closure – to forget rather than remember. Certain mortuary art forms, most notably the extravagant

25 New Ireland *malanggan*, are found extensively in European collections, partly because they are disposed of through sale, unless appropriately destroyed, once their ritual function has been accomplished.

    The loss of salient information is especially notable in eastern Polynesia, where much depopulation and disruption occurred in the nineteenth century, and where understandings of religious practices draw mainly on remembered or orally transmitted information obtained well after conversion to Christianity. While these traditions

34

28 Fish with script combining traditional and introduced characters, Rapanui, 1925. L. 11 in.

may be rich and precise, indigenous converts inevitably see their parents' or ancestors' beliefs through Christian spectacles. It is not therefore surprising to read that figures of principal Polynesian deities, such as Tangaroa, were 'worshipped', and not always easy to say how accurate or inaccurate such statements are. While sacrifices were certainly made in the vicinity of such carvings, they were not objects of devotion in the Western sense.

The most rewarding understanding of the meanings of Oceanic art frequently depends upon a rich contextual knowledge: this knowledge is often either not available or only partly available, making grounded speculation necessary in any enlivening interpretation of museum pieces that have been abstracted from their contexts. What may be crucial is not merely an ethnographic record of the broad pattern of life in the society which produced the work, and some sense of the links between object and subject referred to (for example, shields and deities), but a deeper understanding of ideas about knowledge, work, art and the elements that constitute the individual. In relation to such notions, art forms were usually not looked at with the kind of detached contemplation that seems to characterize the Western viewer's observation of works in art museums; they were rather *used* to effect certain accomplishments: to parade a particular form of power, to overwhelm others, or to overwhelm oneself. While Western art might be seen primarily as a system of meaningful codes, Pacific art suggests that efficacious presentation is generally more important than communication or meaning. The dissimilarities with Western perceptions should not, however, be exaggerated: the fact that Easter Islanders employed a kind of writing system indicates that graphic codification was important to them, and further suggests that it was present to at least a muted degree in the related Polynesian cultures, even though their artifacts were not usually inscribed with meanings in this literal sense.

While the understanding of context is crucial, the questions of what counts as a context, and how it relates to the art objects, are not always simple. Pacific art objects typically work within a number of over-lapping and sometimes contentious contexts within and between soci-eties, rather than in one only. Art forms are important in general, surely, because they do not merely reflect political relationships and cultural categories: new expressions inevitably redefine what is expressed, and may wilfully and artfully overturn hierarchies and cat-egories. This is most conspicuous in critical postcolonial art, which rejects the sovereignty of Western culture and presents new narratives of colonial history, but it is also true, in different ways and on a more localized scale, of art in 'traditional' milieux: the difference is that dispute about political relationships (for example, levels of seniority within a male cult) is likely to be invisible or inexplicable to an outside viewer.

The most regrettable stereotype concerning tribal societies is the idea that indigenous knowledge is dominated by the reproduction and perpetuation of tradition. This would deny the interpretation and innovation always present in Pacific cultures. Meanings were not simply there to be expressed in art forms; artists instead always had to use their imagination when responding to available traditions. To do so was not to express the unique personal creativity that is fetishized in Western understandings of artistic originality, but to interpret and reinvent meaning routinely. Both the continuation of existing tradi-tions and a degree of departure from them is inherent in any cultural production. What varies is the degree to which different cultures value innovation and replication, and the consequent privileging of one aspect or other of particular works, regardless of any 'actual' mix of novelty and reproduction. Hence we might overemphasize changes on the surface, neglecting a deeper conformity with traditional art that is more important in the eyes of a work's producers. But we can also make the mistake of singling out the continuities and neglecting the wit and irony of innovative Oceanic forms. Oceanic art often surprises us, but it is vital to remember that its makers used it to surprise them-selves and each other.

CHAPTER ONE

Revelations: Sepik Art

The Sepik region of northern New Guinea has long been renowned for the richness and diversity of its artistic traditions, and in this regard epitomizes Melanesia as a whole. In the wider region, the proliferation of cultural forms and expressions is marked in languages and social institutions as well as in material culture; the causes of this degree of diversity present an intriguing, if somewhat intractable, problem.

The elaboration of performance, the range of sculpture and decorated material culture, and the variety of basic techniques and approaches to decoration, is certainly remarkable. Eastern Sepik art forms include decorated objects in everyday use – betel mortars, lime containers and spatulae, hangers, cooking pots and food bowls. Spears, arrows and head-hunting canoes were not merely implements to inflict violence, but artfully elaborated devices; the distinction that we might make between their functions and decorative value was probably not clear to their producers. What we take as aesthetic elaboration they very likely took as enhancing the efficacy of weapons, as the adornment of houses and bodies enhanced their efficacy in other ways. Shields were broadly similar to those in other parts of New Guinea (see Chapter 3 for the Asmat) in the sense that dynamic, loosely symmetrical patterns and anthropomorphic figures were carved in low relief and painted, sometimes with the addition of plant fibre tassels and feathers. The objects that are most conspicuous in collections and

29 (below) Ornamental spatula for lime, which is consumed with betel nut in many parts of New Guinea and the Solomon Islands. L. 21¾ in.

30 (right) Club, Massim region, New Guinea. Ht 39⅜ in.

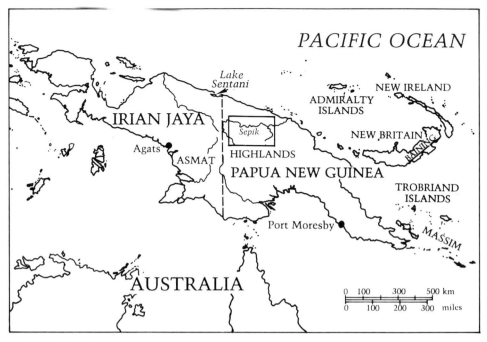

31 Map of New Guinea.

32 The Sepik region and its peoples.

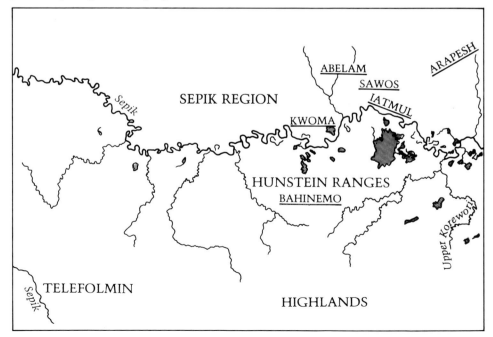

33 Young Iatmul boy with conus disc armrings and shell necklaces, East Sepik, New Guinea, *c.* 1931–2.

34 (*right*) Old Iatmul men impersonating *wagan* (water spirits), whose voices are represented by the beating of slit gongs; the fishing net they carry, with a wooden fish tied to the bottom, raises the *wagan* from the water, *c.* 1931–2.

35 A Sepik initiation: the masked figure waving the staff moves along a row of initiates poised on a canoe hull, ready for scarification, *c.* 1931–2.

36 (*above left*) Mask used in male initiation ceremonies, Kwoma, Sepik, collected 1966. Ht 67¾ in.

37 (*above right*) Mask, Vokeo, Little Schouten Islands, coast of Sepik Province, collected 1934. Ht 19¼ in.

that have received most scholarly attention are, however, those most obviously connected with cult activities, such as sacred flutes, slit gongs, ceremonial stools, ancestral or spirit figures, dance costumes and masks that are carved or made variously of woven basketry, palm spathes, pottery, shells, feathers and paint.

46,47 Elaborate ceremonial houses that incorporate paintings are fundamentally important for cult activities in a number of ways: their insides 36–8 are secret sacred spaces, their gable paintings and masks overshadow the public phases of ceremonies and they are repositories for cult paraphernalia that women and uninitiated males may not see. As well as what we commonly understand to constitute visual art and architecture – that is, a predominantly static art form – these rituals also involve

38 (*opposite*) Abwan mask, Kararau village, Iatmul, central Sepik, collected 1963. Ht 40⅛ in.

35   body decoration, the impersonation of warriors and spirits, the preparation, decoration and consumption of food, sometimes the singing or recitation of narratives, and frequently certain forms of bodily mutilation and ritual violence. Artistic expression is thus not limited to a particularly rich material culture alone, but performs an enormous range of sensory expressions and experiences, which are meaningfully and aesthetically charged.

The degree of diversity may be underlined by the fact that virtually no generalization about Sepik art can be sustained. There are certainly
7   recurring features, such as extended phallic noses, that are widely attested to; but even, say, the observation that anthropomorphic sculpture dramatically exaggerates the face and head, which would be banal and no less true of much other Pacific material, is contradicted by the naturalistic proportions of the human figures that provide the backs to
39   some Iatmul ceremonial seats, of Yuat River figures said to represent 'culture heroes' and of some human-figure suspension hooks. The range of sculptural techniques, including not only carving but many kinds of wicker and fibre assembly, and the addition of clay with inlaid shell, is impressive. The products are sometimes fully in the round, sometimes flattish works to be seen from the front, and sometimes intelligible only in profile; but there are also masks (notably those of the Bahinemo people of the Hunstein ranges south of the Sepik) that incorporate both features that can only be appreciated from the front and those that can only be effective from the side; it is therefore impossible to grasp the whole from one vantage point at any one moment. Decoration incorporates dentate triangles, zigzags, flowing curvilinear forms, concentric circles, and occasionally lines of dots and radiating or parallel stripes. Not only do design elements differ, but there are basic differences in the logic of design, in the sense that in some cases a multiplicity of colours and textures contributes to the effect, while in others a binary contrast between a light outline and dark background is crucial. All this is in complete contrast with other rich Pacific traditions, such as Maori art, which was richly elaborated and similarly extended to an extraordinary range of architectural elements, utensils and weapons, but which was far more coherent in techniques and motifs (see Chapter 2).

Images on objects in public use – that is, those not connected with the male cult – may be readily identified as totems associated with particular descent groups. In many cases, however, figures on paintings and carvings are not named and may merge into polysemous motifs, which men are often unwilling or unable to identify; anthropologists

39 (*left*) Iatmul ceremonial stool with opossum fur, photographed *in situ*, *c* 1931–2.

40 (*above*) Swordfish mask, Kararau, Iatmul, central Sepik, collected 1912–13. L. 7ft ⅝ in.

seeking names and meanings appear to raise questions that do not occur to the painters and carvers themselves, for some art forms, if not all. Because stylistic devices and traits have frequently spread from one region to another, questions of meaning are moreover complicated by the combination of what appears original and what has been adapted. Sometimes a myth accompanying a form may travel with it, in which case a common meaning may be sustained, but in others reference may be diminished and the design element elaborated primarily for its aesthetic effect, or for a new meaning that was not previously apparent. In other words, a process of transposition and translation occurred, or rather one of free translation, given the degree to which motifs and styles have been placed in new contexts to new effect.

43

41 (*above*) Yipwon figure, Yimar,
Upper Korewori, Sepik.
Ht 46 in.

42 (*right*) Fighting shield, Abau,
upper Sepik. 66½ × 23⅜ in.

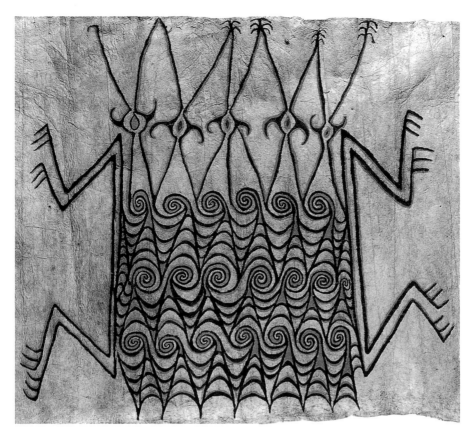

43 Barkcloth, Lake Sentani, Irian Jaya, collected 1926. L. 68⅞ in.

Hooks that are vertically symmetrical, for example, are especially conspicuous in carvings from the upper Korewori River, but are present to varying degrees in other parts of the Sepik. They echo facial features in some contexts, and birds' beaks in others, but do not appear to possess the same connotations in all areas; in other words, the form is fluid and is re-created through association with different figures in different places. In some cases, too, a style such as this may be valued because it marks a cross-cultural exchange relationship and is taken to be emblematic of the group from whom it was obtained. Abelam paintings, for example, were imitated by near neighbours such as the Arapesh, who were probably in awe of Abelam ritual art and power,

41

and may moreover have been threatened by their aggression and expansion. Sculptures might be obtained through trade or styles copied by a group that did not unequivocally admire the exporting culture, but acknowledged its strength and perhaps sought to assimilate itself to it or appropriate some of what seemed to make it expressive and spiritually powerful. Trade and imitation may therefore provide a partial explanation of the proliferation of art forms: if importing groups are steadily acquiring the distinctive art forms of exporting groups, and at the same time creating new local variants, the latter may be stimulated to produce novel styles and types that sustain their distinctiveness.

The process of transposition can be seen to have taken place on a larger geographical scale, though its political context no doubt varied considerably. A motif that could be seen as a flattened or split transformation of the hooks, more typically carved in low relief, painted or modelled in clay, is based around concentric arcs that echo a circle and that are generally confined within a triangular space that may be part of a larger zigzag. Each sequence of arcs is then juxtaposed with another tending the opposite way, towards a dynamism that can be 42 remarkably powerful, as in the upper Sepik shield from the Green or Idam River that is now in Basel. Though sometimes more rigid and symmetrical, the effect in general is to accentuate features and convey a sense of vigour in anthropomorphic and animal figures. On pottery and some woodcarving, this design tends to be constructed around eyes, and it might be presumed that even where circles are not obviously paired, it does connote a face (though a bird's eye and beak is also suggested in the shield, and arcs of this type also appear all over the 'bodies' of anthropomorphic carvings that serve as cornerposts in some ceremonial houses). Further afield, this recurs as a conspicuous 43 element to the west in Lake Sentani barkcloth and in carvings from 30 the same area, and in the Massim to the south-east. In these cases, the facial association seems to be absent and it can only be assumed that the pattern was borrowed in one direction or the other simply because it was technically efficacious; it does not possess a meaning or referent but rather *does* something – that is, it visually invigorates a spirit, a human, or perhaps a crocodile or bird.

Populations such as the Abelam and Arapesh, who live in the hills at some remove from the Sepik River itself, subsist on yams and sago and place great ritual emphasis on yam fertility and harvest; for them, and for smaller middle Sepik groups, such as the Kwoma, the yam is carefully and laboriously nurtured by men and protected from

46

44 Iatmul crocodile mask, mounted on the front of a canoe, *c.* 1931–2.

'contamination' by women, or rather by the reproductive capacities that women appear to represent. Not only are contacts with yam gardens taboo, especially to women who are menstruating or have recently given birth, but men and their wives observe prohibitions on sexual activity; even men whose wives are pregnant are believed to be weakened and must not touch sacred objects related to the yam cult. Harvest ceremonies involve making sculptures and painting and displaying the yams, which are subsequently given away in competitive presentations. Given the effort, skill and elaboration, and the identifications between patently phallic, long yams and their growers, these products are clearly works of art in themselves, and were aptly described as a form of 'vegetable sculpture' by Anthony Forge, who studied the Abelam in the 1950s and 1960s and who wrote a number of essays of fundamental importance for the interpretation of Sepik art, which have been drawn upon in this chapter.

Because the grower is believed to invest his own blood into his yams, he cannot eat them himself; this would be a form of 'incestuous' consumption that would result in serious disease or death, and

45 Painting from a ceremonial house, Keram river, lower Sepik, collected 1930. Ht 42½ in.

conforms with prohibitions upon a man eating a pig that he has speared or reared. Elsewhere in New Guinea, a work of art, a nurtured animal or dish of food may be identified with a user or recipient rather than with the thing's producer (weapons, in particular, are likely to bear the person of the warrior rather than the craftsman who has carved them). In the case of the yams, the idea of creation might seem closer to a Western notion of authorship in that the maker is projected into the product; this would also appear true of the paintings which Arapesh initiators prepare and present to the younger men they are sponsoring. The artist is supposed to project his indwelling spirit into the painting (usually of an ambiguously sexed spirit and totemic birds) and bestow it upon the man who then also acquires the named spirit, until he in turn transmits it, through a painting of his own, to a novice at a later stage in the cycle of initiations (the fact that a master artist may provide considerable assistance to the man defined as the painter does not matter; the painting is understood to emanate from the latter rather than from the former).

This draws attention to the way in which art works and other products have distinct, culturally specified lives. Their uses are in one sense political and economic (as men move up through a hierarchy based on age and ritual knowledge and yams are circulated and eaten), but they carry elements of people in particular ways, and these associations define how the art objects are valued, circulated, displayed and consumed. For both yams and paintings, the investment of the creator in the creation does not result in any kind of natural possession (which Western perceptions of authorship might anticipate): on the contrary, the creation must be given away. The difference between these cases and that of the weapon closely identified with the warrior (and possibly also with a renowned warrior-ancestor) reminds us that there is no total 'non-Western', 'Melanesian' or even general Sepik model of how art forms and other products are identified and circulated. Differences between one society and the next, or between the treatment of paintings and the treatment of shields within the one society, may entail models of identification that differ in principle in the same way that the Western art market differs in principle from the gift and kinship systems in which non-Western art forms are embedded. The most important aspect is what the art practices are understood to accomplish: what makes yam-growing a matter of politicized aesthetic expression, rather than merely a subsistence operation, is the enhancement of a spiritually empowered masculinity to the exclusion or apparent exclusion of women.

46 (*left*) Tambaran house facade paintings, Apangai village, East Sepik, 1979.

47 (*below*) Tambaran house, Sepik, 1979.

River people such as the Iatmul and Sawos do not grow yams, but another cult, which is also highly elaborated among the Arapesh and Abelam, is a similar vehicle for the creation and re-creation of masculinity. What is called the Tambaran in pidgin is a complex of graded male initiation rites that dramatize sexual difference and overtly wean boys and men away from maternal influences. Much more than a one-off event marking puberty, these grades constitute a whole hierarchy beginning at infancy, and are staged through various phases of adolescence, maturity and old age. Unlike the graded society of north Vanuatu, in which some but not all men achieve higher rank individually as they bring pigs appropriate for sacrifice to maturity, or in some cases obtain necessary quantities of pigs through exchange, the Sepik ideal is that all men should progress through the grades in sets based on generation and kin classifications – though in both areas finding the resources to feed sponsors and manufacture necessary art works and structures is a difficult accomplishment and a context for competition.

Initiation at each phase generally takes the form of some kind of terror or ordeal, after which novices are shown the secret sacred objects or musical instruments associated with the grade. Through most of its stages, the cult is closely connected with a ceremonial house erected either specifically for Tambaran rites or used in a longer-term way as a men's house. These houses, renowned for their paintings on coconut- or sago-spathe, are particularly splendid among the Abelam, where the facade may rise as much as twenty-five to thirty metres from the ground. Arapesh *haus* Tambaran are smaller but nevertheless impressive, at around fifteen to eighteen metres high, while those in the upper Sepik are often smaller. Iatmul houses are large but have a saddle-shaped roof line and substantial facade paintings at both ends. Among some people such as the Kwoma, the houses are more open; there is no facade, but paintings cover the interior of the roof and are displayed around the main supporting poles. Houseposts and beams are carved into anthropomorphic figures identified with spirits and mythological characters, while paintings mostly refer to plant and animal totems, which belong to particular kin groups and can only be painted by them.

The very size of Abelam and Arapesh houses is important not simply because their magnificence expresses clan prestige, but because their construction requires efforts of co-ordination and technical feats of extraordinary difficulty. Tall and heavy cornerposts are raised and dropped into deep holes, and a ridgebeam that may weigh a ton is hoisted and shouldered up temporary central poles to the height of the roof line. These operations, which can only proceed once spirits have been introduced into the village and a whole series of preparations, feasts and rites of purification have been made, are mostly carried out through bursts of intensive and highly co-ordinated work. In the case of the ridgepole, the task is begun in the half-light of early morning and is ideally completed before women and children get up; they are then told that the accomplishment is that of the spirit, and even if they do not believe this, both they and the men themselves must sense that this sudden, collective achievement is so removed from ordinary forms of work and social relationships that it is no less miraculous. At another phase of the Arapesh ritual cycle, the mock hamlet of Wamwinipux is constructed in the bush; all the materials are carefully brought together in advance, so that when the actual house-building begins, it proceeds at an extraordinary pace: 'the effect sought is to have Wamwinipux seemingly rise before one's eyes in the forest' (D. Tuzin, *The Voice of the Tambaran*). Men are amazed by achievements of this kind; the products of their efforts are at one moment so remarkable that they appear magical, yet the magic revealed is that of human action. The art forms of the Tambaran house and mockhamlet are not images or reflections of society, but images created by men, which enable them to see their own creativity, and a kind of sociality that has to be continually projected and reinvented, because it does not otherwise exist.

Among the Iatmul, the Abelam and the Arapesh, the houses and associated art forms combine male and female symbolism in various ways. The ridgepole is a phallic form and is associated with yams, spears and warfare, while the house as a whole – among the Abelam but not the Arapesh – is understood as a female form, its interior being equated with the belly. Arapesh and Abelam paintings, however, depict spirits that possess both male and female characteristics and in some cases the penis itself is rendered as a source of nurture, a provider of semen, analogous to the milk-yielding breast.

This epitomizes the sense in which the enhancement of masculinity is based paradoxically upon the mimicry of female creativity in art forms that are kept secret from real women. As is discussed further in Chapter 5, in relation to the central Highlands people whose beliefs and practices are in many ways similar to those of the Sepik, initiation imitates birth and can be seen to involve some appropriation of female powers by men. In the Abelam and Arapesh cases, the recurrence of deception is especially striking in situations where novices can hear or see the spirit, which is then revealed to be merely a man playing a whistle, bamboo flute or slit gong. Throughout rituals, women are

48 Cornerpost of a ceremonial house, representing a wood spirit, Palimbai, Iatmul, East Sepik, *c.* 1931–2.

49 Hoisting the massive ridgepole of a ceremonial house in East Sepik, Papua New Guinea, 1971. The man holding the pale-coloured pole on the right touches the ridgepole with a magic bundle in an effort to reduce its weight.

told that food for initiates will be eaten by the spirit, that men hunting pigs will chase and seize the spirit, that boys taken to a secluded mockvillage are transformed into flying foxes, and so on. The novices who actually eat, hunt or undergo seclusion are let into the secret and led to understand that at some metaphorical or imagistic level, the food is in essence consumed by the spirit in the same way that they 'become' flying foxes.

53

These contrivances are profoundly risky, particularly because not only women but novices are deceived, and though the latter alone are undeceived in turn, the structure of revelation is such that any truth subsequently revealed may turn out to be a further contrivance. The possibility that the great spirit Nggwal is only 'what men do' is explicitly countenanced by some informants, according to Donald Tuzin's work among the Arapesh (though in other contexts, the same speakers express real fear of the spirit's malevolent efficacy). 'What men do', however, is not some practical trickery that is devoid of the work of the Tambaran, but a tentative effort of collective sociality. The initiation rites do not merely take boys away from their mothers – often in spectacularly violent ways – and make them into individual men: they also make collectivities of men, who can understand their mutual selfhood as a larger, objectified, glorious entity. The probable infrequency of these rites, even in traditional times, the difficulty and conflict involved in organizing them, and their dormant or defunct state in many areas today, however, establishes that this male collective sociality, which a Western person might take to be as self-evidently real as the Tambaran is unreal, is a fragile rhetorical contrivance of the same order.

The prominence of secrecy suggests that the widespread belief that art expresses broader cultural values is not quite appropriate for the Sepik. The rites, art forms and beliefs associated with the cult rest uneasily with classic definitions of culture that emphasize the *shared* nature of ideas and values. There might be common responses to much public imagery, but knowledge connected with the Tambaran is powerful precisely because it is *not* shared: one might even be forgiven for thinking that the fact that women are excluded is more important than the thing from which they are excluded. Even among the men, degrees of knowledge are highly differentiated, since what pertains to any particular stage of initiation is on the one hand unavailable to those who have not reached that point, and on the other superceded or encompassed by the revelations obtained by those at a higher stage.

This is not to say that there is nothing like 'culture' in the Sepik, in the sense that there are broader understandings concerning the ways in which spirits enable growth and cause harm, the way in which magic is effected, and the way in which taboos ensure that the men's projects are insulated from the power and danger of women's bodies and menstrual blood, as women and babies are insulated from the power and danger of magical paint. Some art forms are closely connected with these beliefs, although the facade paintings are associated

54

50 (*opposite*) Facade painting from an Abelam house, central Sepik. Ht 64⅞ in.

with spiritual power in a general way rather than being representative of specific spirits. The art forms that are exclusive to the cult might also be said to express the broader animistic view of the world, but really only do so to the degree that these perceptions broadly frame ritual practices. It would seem more true to say that objects such as masks amount to a kind of rhetoric that enhances male identity; this is a delicate and deceptive practice that is energized, yet constantly prejudiced, by its own successive demystifications.

Musical instruments are important among the sacred cult art forms, as has been noted; while museums assimilate these to the class of masks and carvings by emphasizing their visual characteristics, it may be more helpful to reverse the operation and consider masks as functioning like gongs and flutes. One may certainly say that a decorated instrument expresses something of the culture that produced it, but this is plainly less important than the fact that it changes the aural environment – sometimes very dramatically. Similarly, the sudden appearance of masks, the shock of the sight of a newly constructed hamlet in the forest, or the look of a highly decorated man might startle as powerfully as a sudden noise (and the appearances of these images would, of course, mostly be accompanied by some music or chanting). This, it could be suggested, is more important than apparent symbolic resonances with what might be taken to be broader cultural values. The total view may be sought by an outside interpreter such as an anthropologist, and indeed has value as an interpretable fiction that enables us, the Western viewer, to imagine meanings and systems in certain ways; but we should not presume that this type of cultural analysis has any counterpart in indigenous perceptions: such systematizations, like maps that only strangers need, are simply unlikely to be relevant to the way art works are produced and responded to.

It is intriguing that in most Sepik languages there is no vernacular term for the whole ensemble of cult practices: Tambaran is a pidgin word now widely used in the area. It is tempting to suggest that the introduction of Christianity and various new cargo cults, which presented themselves as total alternate systems, made what was previously a series of related rites more visible as a whole 'cult'. The question of how the whole is made explicit is linked with an issue that has preoccupied a number of anthropologists in the Sepik: that is, the degree to which those engaged in producing art and ritual appear unconcerned with the 'meanings' of their works and their reluctance to explain or interpret them.

This is most marked among the Abelam and suggests that art, especially painting, is not a medium through which narratives and beliefs that exist otherwise are expressed, as Christian painting in the West refers to and depends upon Biblical knowledge. Nor is Abelam art a kind of visual translation of oral religious lore or mythology; it is expressive in itself rather than being a vehicle for communication. The Abelam do not possess an elaborate corpus of mythology; in fact myth is virtually non-existent among them, and the body of linguistic knowledge that anthropologists would elsewhere seek to relate closely to art is thus simply not there. Anthropological interpretation cannot, in this case, aim to arrive at the indigenous 'meanings' of art forms, because the art is effective within dramatic situations: it contributes to the aura and power of staged events, but does not implicitly contain the kind of discourse that a Western reading might uncover.

The situation among the Arapesh is somewhat different in the sense that there is a corpus of mythology that deals with relations between the sexes and the power of spirits, among other matters. It is intriguing that the Tambaran and associated art forms appear to have been adopted by Arapesh society (at a relatively late date) from the Abelam, given that their culture made much use of myth, and that the play of deception and revelation appears peculiarly fraught among them. The paradoxes of male self-fashioning, in other words, may be more easily sustained if there is no exegesis – if images are simply produced rather than talked about, or articulated and translated between visual and verbal genres such as art and myth. If men not only imitated female procreativity but told themselves that this is what they were doing, confronting the paradox as a verbalized paradox rather than an unstated effect, the rhetoric might be more self-defeating than self-energizing.

51 Bowl, Marquesas Islands. Ht 5 in., Diam. 12 in.

CHAPTER TWO

Ancestors and Architecture: Maori Art

In Maori conceptions of time, it is said, the past is before one and the future behind: people therefore face their ancestors, even as they experience a linear succession of changes. This is not to say that Maori were backward-looking or in a condition of cultural stasis. On the contrary, before colonization, Maori society was competitive and dynamic and so it has remained; although distinctions of rank between chiefs and commoners existed, sanctity and status were expressed and validated through performance, and warfare often resulted in dramatic changes in social geography.

Maori art, moreover, represents an innovative and dramatic departure from the traditions with which it is most closely related. The ancestors of Tahitians, Maori, Marquesans, Hawaiians and other eastern Polynesians lived in the Marquesas or Society Islands and went separate ways only at a late stage in the history of Oceanic settlement. The Maori migrated by canoe from tropical Polynesia to the cooler and much larger islands, later named New Zealand, around a thousand years ago. While fish-hooks, adzes and a range of other artifacts with many common cultural features, establish that Maori art developed from an eastern Polynesian base, the discontinuities are more striking than the similarities. Most noticeably, the curvilinear element, which can be traced back to Lapita designs and recurs in combination with rectilinear forms in eastern Polynesian carving, is emphasized and extended relentlessly in Maori art.

The sheer elaboration and extent of design is also conspicuous: ancestral figures and utensils in Tahiti, such as food dishes, tend to lack surface decoration, whereas a great variety of Maori architectural forms, canoes, weapons, containers and implements are densely and intricately carved. Although increasingly elaborate ornamentation over the colonial period was clearly made possible by new tools and perhaps encouraged by new aesthetic influences, dense decoration was certainly also particularly characteristic of work in wood even before contact with Europeans. The curvilinear motifs were also reproduced in tattooing and painting, and in some carving in other media, but

51

52 Carved and painted house, called Wairarapa.

bone and greenstone were generally handled with greater austerity, and woven flax cloaks were similarly understated. Some changes were stimulated or compelled by distinctive features of the New Zealand environment – the greater range of timber and stone, as well as the unsuitability of the climate for the trees generally used to make bark-cloth – but Maori innovation went far beyond mere adaptation.

The point that Maori faced their ancestors rather than the future is important, not because the culture was tradition-bound, but because genealogy and ancestral presences were sources of empowerment in the present. Genealogies were recited ritually in a whole range of contexts, such as at the birth and naming of children, and were crucial in disputes concerning rights to land and resources. Ancestors were and are most conspicuous in the large houses on tribal meeting-grounds (*marae*). The 'great house', or *wharenui*, developed during the early nineteenth century through the elaboration of elements that seem to have been already present in the houses of prominent chiefs.

Like both ordinary dwellings and collective or cult houses elsewhere in Oceania, these meeting-houses did not so much represent a social

52,56

60

group as create it as a presence. The whole building symbolized the body of an ancestor: the roof beam was the spine, the rafters the ribs and the barge boards in the front the arms; the depth of the metaphorical scheme in the ancestral Polynesian cultures is marked by a creation chant from the Society Islands recorded in 1822, in which the paramount deity Ta'aroa was said to be 'a god's house; his backbone was the ridgepole, his ribs were the supporters.' This was not, however, a neat code that extended to other elements, which, both on the facade and internally, are primarily carvings of individual ancestors –

53 (*below left*) *Pou tokomanawa*, ancestor figure from a meeting-house of Tumoanakotore, Mamaku, Hicks Bay, collected 1910. Ht 54⅜ in.

54 (*below right*) *Poupou* in the style of the Te Arawa.

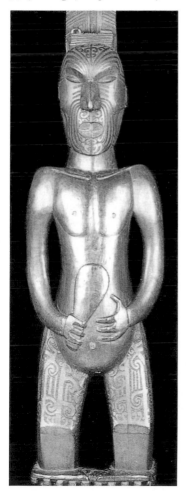

mostly, but not exclusively, male. Those depicted were not necessarily all progenitors in a strict biological sense; others, including Europeans who were historically significant, and perhaps connected to a tribe by marriage or adoption, might also be represented.

53
54
In the house's centre are *pou tokomanawa*, sculptures in the round that support ridgepoles, while *poupou* constitute supporting panels in relief along the walls (and in fact were the walls in older houses). Although most examples in museums are now unpainted or painted red, the nineteenth century saw a good deal of experimentation in the painting of both exterior and interior carving, and figurative painting was in some cases substituted for carving. There was a significant degree of regional variation, but *poupou* are always shown frontally (or rather, in a combination of frontal and split-profile views) and largely symmetrically, with (usually) three-fingered hands across the stomach or chest. While the *pou tokomanawa* are sometimes virtually devoid of surface decoration (though ancestors' tattoos are almost always reproduced), the wall panels are usually densely covered with elaborate motifs and additional figures that overlie and obscure the torso.

Between these carvings are stitched lattice panels or *tukutuku*, bearing geometric designs, and above the *poupou* are rafters painted with intricate and repetitive curvilinear forms in red, white and black. The panels were named on the basis of resemblances to fish, ribs and stars, and *tukutuku* occasionally incorporate images of ancestors or their names in European script, but both these and the rafter patterns more typically express projects of formal experimentation that contrast with the primarily referential character of the sculpture.

From a European perspective, the *pou tokomanawa*, being in the round, frequently appear more naturalistic and individualized than the stylized wall carvings, but both represent individuals and not generic ancestors. The importance of a genealogy inhered not so much in its sheer depth, or in a line of high rank (as was more the case in the highly stratified societies of Hawaii, Tahiti and Tonga) but in a particular history of migrations, battles and incidents from which rights in land, fishing-grounds and other resources derived. Even highly stylized figures frequently bear certain artifacts, tattoos and other distinctive traits, or are represented with accompanying figures – occasionally even a dog – that would have identified them as individuals to members of the extended family or tribe.

Although these carvings are representational, they do more than evoke or recall the absent dead. On the *marae* (the location of tribal belonging and sociality, formerly in chiefs' houses), carvings can instead be seen to create ancestors as real and immediate presences. The solidity of the wood itself expresses hardness and substance, and even the patina of decaying carving suggests the extended, multiple life cycles through which particular families and tribes trace their descent. The surface decoration also has particular effect, which goes beyond the ornamental: the elaborate spiral forms, the tubular bodies of certain regional styles and the almost tortuous density of pattern, convey energy and movement and a kind of continuing vitality that a mere image of a dead person could not possess. The generative capacity of the ancestor is frequently attested to by additional figures between the legs or across the chest, representing a wife and children; the sense of action is reinforced by the projecting tongue, marking the *haka* or ritualized challenge, appropriate to both warfare and formal greeting ceremonies. Maori art does not seem to create 'images' of people that are less substantial than the people themselves; instead it produces embodiments that surround the activities of the meeting-house and *marae* as a whole. Ancestors were there to bear upon debates about collective action in war, and action in relation to Europeans, as they bore witness to the transmission of tribal knowledge, the mourning of the dead and to moments of interaction between the people of a *marae* and guests from other groups.

Meeting-houses were elaborated over a period of instability and dramatic change, as contact with Europeans led both to conflict with them, and intensified conflict among the Maori themselves. New weapons and alliances occasioned warfare on a larger scale, often with the aim of dispossessing other groups; all-out war no doubt took place before European contact, but more limited feuding, which did not severely disrupt subsistence and other activities, was probably more typical. Under these circumstances, meetings with both Europeans and other Maori no doubt became more frequent, and often addressed issues of profound difficulty and importance. The visual and experiential effect of the meeting-house needs to be seen both as a challenge to those foreigners, allies and potential enemies who visited, often under tense and uneasy circumstances, and as a source of affirmation for those who identified with its genealogy.

The excess that is arguably present in the elaboration of the carving is important in this context. The viewer's eye moves between the whole figure and its constitutive forms: it is drawn around particular motifs, and from one spiral to another, into the play between spirals and their interstitial chevrons and dentate forms. A focused grasp of the whole carving is perceptually difficult; this optical complexity and restlessness reinforces the awe-inspiring effect that is certainly often intended by expressions of challenge and defiance. These figures cannot be gazed upon with any confidence; they tend rather to crowd out the viewer's own sense of presence and power. The viewer who identifies genealogically with the figure can move beyond this state of uncertainty, because he or she ideally recapitulates the ancestors' *mana* (power) and efficacy; what may be initially confusing and threatening can be recognized as the ancestral source of the self, and can be incorporated into it. Outsiders, on the other hand, are excluded from this positive dynamic of self-definition, and are likely to be at least intimidated; whether they feel threatened and estranged or merely awed would no doubt depend on the state of relations between them and their hosts. Carvings clearly intended to threaten rather than to impress alone must include the ancestral warriors that were built into the palisades of fortified villages. These figures, often bearing a hand club and an erect penis, evoked not only the prowess of the group, but probably also specific narratives concerning the warriors depicted, who might in the past have assaulted or terrorized the same enemies they again confronted.

55 *Pataka*, Lake Taupo, 1878. 6⅞ × 10¾ in.

56 Meeting-house of Hotunui.

55   The storehouses, called *pataka*, were built to protect heirloom valuables and important food stores, such as preserved fish, from thieves and rats. They, like meeting-houses, were elaborately carved and painted, though not internally, but on the facade and sides. Until the early nineteenth century, these rather than meeting-houses were the focal points of tribal prestige; as agriculture changed to incorporate new crops, and as new kinds of wealth became significant, they declined in importance as the meeting-houses became more central. Although ancestors are depicted along the side walls of the Te Puawai storehouse in the Auckland museum, this is unusual, and the most conspicuous figures on the front sideposts and above the central door were usually couples engaged in sexual intercourse: the immediate impression relates not to the destructive threat of a particular warrior or the cumulative strength of a whole line of ancestors, but to the generative capacities and fecundity of a chief or his extended family. This opulence was also attested to simply by the size and elaboration of the structure and by what it might be known or

57 expected to contain. In some cases the barge boards that constitute an inverted *V* carried representations of whales or some other large sea creatures being dragged ashore, reinforcing the theme of abundant harvest. Spirals and a range of other motifs similar to those in meeting-house carvings also appeared on the facades and side walls of these structures.

    Given that the lattice panels in meeting-houses are made by women, and the carvings by men, and that a pair of male and female ancestors are frequently conspicuous in the facade, the house seems divided between male and female elements. The structuralist argument that all cultures are organized in terms of binary oppositions becomes contrived if its implications are pursued too far, but oppositions between male and female, raw and cooked, right and left, and life and death indeed seem fundamental in Maori culture. In particular, the active union of male and female in any creative or productive activity was continually emphasized in mythology and ritual: the origins of the world in the conjuncture of earth and sky, the planting of the staple, sweet potato, and the making of ritual fire, were all operations understood in explicitly sexual terms. Men and women did not, however, actually work together; the building and carving of meeting-houses and canoes, and certain other practices, such as tattooing, were intensely *tapu* (taboo); carvers and other specialists were therefore segregated, as cooked food and women were excluded from the structures under construction. Women's

66

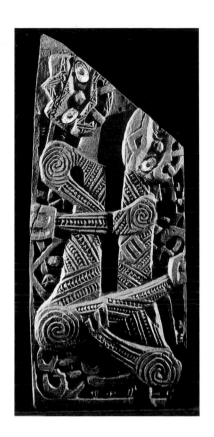

57 Barge board support from a *pataka* named Te Awhi. Ht 29¼ in.

creative efforts were surrounded by their own *tapu*, and in all cases – tattooing, house building and weaving – the condition of sanctity was ritually removed upon the completion of the task. Generative sexual union was typically depicted on the ridgepole over the porch in meeting-houses, as it was in the storehouses, but more generally the combination of male and female work gives material form to a larger ideal of sexual complementarity.

There are many issues concerning stylistic variation in meeting-houses, their historical development and their changing meanings in rural and urban areas that might be explored further. In general, however, the coherence of the architecture, the prominence of ancestors, and the significance of the built space in social life, can be readily perceived; on the other hand, certain architectural elements and carved figures have proven peculiarly difficult to interpret.

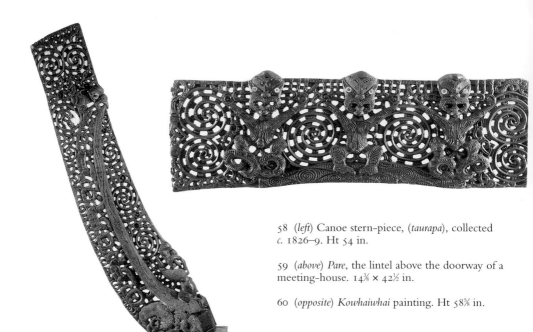

58 (*left*) Canoe stern-piece, (*taurapa*), collected
c. 1826–9. Ht 54 in.

59 (*above*) *Pare*, the lintel above the doorway of a
meeting-house. 14⅜ × 42½ in.

60 (*opposite*) *Kowhaiwhai* painting. Ht 58⅝ in.

There is a class of fantastic hybrid figures, known as *manaia*, that
incorporate, sometimes in highly stylized forms, human, reptilian and
bird-like features; they are frequently in a contorted posture, or in one
of attack, and actually bite into unambiguously human figures,
although this may imply a transfer of *mana* rather than aggression.
They occur in much sculpture, including some *poupou* carvings, canoe
59 stern-pieces, and most strikingly in *pare* (lintels) above meeting-house
doorways. The lizard is generally a conspicuous, if not a dominant
element, and as lizards were generally bad omens and signs of illness
and death, it might be speculated that the juxtaposition of sinuous and
contorted *manaia* figures with human forms in the lintels dramatizes
the opposition of life and death. This would not, however, explain the
fact that the sea-creatures on storehouses are dragged ashore by *manaia,*
who therefore seem to be providing food for people, rather than
threatening them, or otherwise signifying their malaise. Nor would
such a direct identification with death seem consistent with the *manaia*
across the chests and shoulders of some ancestors in *poupou* panels; the
figures in this case appear to be associated with humans in a complementary, or at least benign way, and thus must possess contextual rather
than unambiguously negative significance.

In general, an excessively literal approach to symbolism, which takes particular components of carving or motifs to stand for mythological personae, incidents or themes in a regular way, probably diminishes the expressive effect that art forms possessed in their contexts. Both European ethnologists and some Maori have been inclined to codify Maori culture into a body of folklore that can be readily described and taught, and through which definite meanings can be ascribed to carvings. It has been suggested, for instance, that lintels, which frequently incorporate one or more human figures with upraised arms, represent the god Tane who pushed apart the original parents, Rangi and Papa (sky and earth), until then locked together in copulation, stifling their six sons. Tane's action was certainly cosmologically fundamental, in that it opened the way for a succession of further creative acts and for human life in general, but the event certainly cannot be represented in all lintels, which sometimes depict female figures, and often two or three figures rather than one. Although the idea that a god might be several rather than one is of basic importance in Polynesian religion, the multiple expressions are differentiated into particular aspects of a deity's persona, rather than each being complete copies of the other. A key aspect of the legend is moreover that Tane alone was successful in separating the parents: from this follows his unique status as the maker of the first woman and the parent of the first man. It has also been argued that lintels include male or female figures in certain positions referring to the three epochs or conditions of the world – nothingness, night and light.

The anthropomorphic figures in lintels may indeed have been identified with particular deities or founding ancestors in some cases, but their overall effect may, most importantly, have stemmed from the combination of personal identifications with the mythological form, within an arrangement that dramatized polarities between life and death. In virtually all cases, there are marked oppositions between human and *manaia* figures, and between these figures and spiral forms. The works, in other words, may have been powerful not because there was a one-to-one correspondence between any or all of these elements and named genealogical characters, but because of the dramatic relationship that implied an array of more particular relationships with humans.

This would be consistent with a broader sense in which Maori art seems not only to present various oppositions and relations of complementarity, but to experiment with the logic of opposition and tension. This is most conspicuous in the treatment of symmetry, especially in

61 Detail of a club,
Marquesas Islands. Ht 54 in.

rafter painting. The most conspicuous element is the *koru* motif,
which consists of a curved line turning in on itself, becoming a circle.
Koru are typically multiplied through branches at the end of imbal-
anced crescent forms and painted in white, the spaces between being
filled in alternately with red and black. *Kowhaiwhai* painting also uses
crescent forms, from which circles have been bitten out, and certain
broken or overlapping spirals, plus a number of other elements, both
separately and in combination with *koru*. Although it is suggested that
the *koru* is based upon a growing fern frond, and the element of growth
and life that that would imply is indeed fundamental, the patterns are
not images of ferns, but primarily non-referential explorations of
symmetry, inversion, growth and transposition. These motifs are
reproduced, generally on a smaller scale, on painted paddles, incised
gourds, in tattooing and less commonly in carving.

In *kowhaiwhai* generally, and especially in earlier nineteenth-century
painting, which tends to be freer than later work, symmetry is

71

frequently disrupted through additional spirals and other elements: through the combination of inversion and direct repetition and through variation in background colouring (one *koru* surrounded by red, its mirror-image by black, for instance). Allan Hanson has suggested that this is a systematic feature of much Maori art, corresponding with a distinctive perception of the world, as pervaded by contradiction and ambivalent tension. This is sustained by the emphasis in mythology on oppositions between earth and sky, life and death, male and female, but is hardly specific to Maori culture alone. Broken 61 symmetry is conspicuous in a number of other Oceanic art traditions – on Trobriand canoe prows, on Marquesan clubs and on ceremonial shields and dance paddles from a number of regions. It suggests that many of these art forms are associated either with actual fighting or competitive exchange and performances in which one side uses visual brilliance to dazzle or disconcert the other. This is clearly the case for Maori warriors' tattoos, and perhaps less obviously, but no less importantly so, for the *wharenui*; as was suggested earlier, the meeting-house is simultaneously the built genealogy of a particular group, and a proud, if not aggressive assertion of that group's *mana* with respect to others.

So far, I have discussed Maori art as though it was uniform. 54 Differing regional styles are in fact conspicuous. Te Arawa *poupou,* produced over the area from Tauranga on the coast to Rotorua and Taupo in the interior, tend to low relief and emphasis upon a V-shaped browridge that sometimes reinforces a deeper *V* formed from pairs of *manaia* figures across the ancestor's chest. Work from the East Cape tends to differentiate the ancestor's body more distinctly from the decoration behind, to emphasize shoulder and knee joints with substantial spirals, and inclines generally to rounder rather than rectilinear forms (although the treatment is still generally frontal and symmetrical). Auckland area carvings, and those from Northland, tend to be still more flowing and sinuous, the torso making an almost tubular form, although rectangular work is more characteristic of the Bay of Islands. Taranaki carving, from the west coast, resembles the northern sinuous style, though heavier spiral forms typically emphasize figures' shoulders, buttocks and knees. The variations are not, however, consistent across most types of carving, let alone between carving and other art forms: figures on lintels from Rotorua, for example, are more rounded than the *poupou* from the same area.

Much of what has been said about *marae* does not apply to the South Island, where the colder climate made the cultivation of sweet potato

62 (*left*) Door frame, Ngati Whatua tribe, Otakanini, between 1500 and 1800. Ht 8 ft ½ in.

63 (*above*) Dendroglyph, Hapupu, east coast, Chatham Islands.

possible only in the coastal area to the north of Banks Peninsula. Populations were generally nomadic and although fortified sites might be resorted to successively over time (as particular localities were occupied seasonally), architecture was obviously of more limited significance. The northern end of the South Island was occupied by invaders including Ngati Toa and Te Ati Awa people, who crossed the strait in the early nineteenth century; the art styles accordingly resembled those of the North Island regions of origin. The largest tribe, the Ngai Tahu, had their own distinctive style; Kati Mamoe carvings were sparsely decorated and more akin to eastern Polynesian than the North Island styles. All these traditions are poorly represented in museum collections.

The complexities of variation in the North Island are compounded both by the movement of individual carvers, who might be working away from their places of origin, and by technical change over the course of the nineteenth century, from stone to iron adzes and then from adzes to chisels. Roger Neich has argued that the substitution of chisels for adzes entailed a new, closer manner of work, a shift to compressed, intricate detail in place of free flow, shallow relief rather than deeper sculpture, and a more pictorial approach to the whole figure. This pictorialism partly reflected the method of work (figures now being sketched out before being carved), but also became more appropriate to a situation in which some traditional knowledge was lost: allusive marks of ancestors' identities were replaced by more explicit representation, and names in European script were sometimes carved across a figure's chest. This trend is taken further in the late

133

64 Tene Waitere at work.

65 Carving of the deity Maui, innovatively represented in oblique profile, fishing up the North Island of New Zealand, by Tene Waitere. This was part of the Rauru meeting-house, carved in 1898–9 for a hotel at Whakarewarewa, which was sold only a few years later to the Hamburg Museum für Völkerkunde, where it is still on display. Ht 7 ft ⅜ in.

nineteenth-century development of figurative painting, which often possesses a definite narrative element, and the prominent display of photographs of elders and ancestors in meeting-houses; however, although in each case there is a radical shift in subject with the change in media, there is an underlying continuity in making a genealogy visible.

The trend to work in a shallower plane was offset by contact-inflenced experimentation on the part of individual carvers, among whom Tene Waitere is especially notable for the incorporation of oblique perspectives without precedent in traditional work. Over the second half of the nineteenth century, carvings were also produced for sale to tourists, for installation in hotels and for showcases of Maori culture in museums and at international expositions. In these cases, the figures depicted were often principal deities such as Maui, whose exploits were popularized through publications of New Zealand folklore, making Maori myth available as an emblem of national distinctiveness, just as the boomerang entered the iconography of white settler identity in Australia. Appropriation of this kind on the

64,65

65

75

part of Europeans did not, however, mark the subordination of Maori art to the dominant settler interest. Even when carving for tourists was engaged in most extensively, the experts continued to work on meeting-houses and on other Maori commissions, and innovations in each context enriched the other. This trend continued into the twentieth century, as urban *marae* were built for migrants from diverse tribal backgrounds: in these cases, too, the founders of the great tribes are more appropriately depicted than recent ancestors who only enter into the genealogies of particular families.

I have emphasized the energetic motion of Maori art, which is marked both in the orchestrated instability of flowing forms, and by transpositions across artifact types and media. It is almost as though motifs had a capacity to replicate themselves on different materials and in different contexts: the *koru* is the key element in rafter painting and on decorated gourds, but appears also in tattooing and carving, and is sometimes painted on other parts of houses and on *pataka*; spiral forms recur in tattooing and many forms of carving, often wholly abstractly, as in the remarkable openwork structures of canoe prows and stern-posts, but can also possess an almost representational character, where solid circles stand for knees or buttocks; and the triangular patterns woven on *taniko* cloaks are reproduced sometimes as a kind of geometric counterpoint to the flow of *koru* on some painted panels. Types of ornaments and implements are moreover exemplified in different media: adzes and chisels are made for utilitarian purposes from a variety of basalts and greenstone or nephrite, but the latter were also of higher status and ceremonial importance. The clubs known as *patu* may be made from stone, greenstone or whalebone; others may be either in bone or wood.

Anthropomorphic ornaments known as *hei tiki* were also made from greenstone, and these and other valuables were passed on at death and sometimes exhumed from burials to be transmitted to descendants. Both personal ornaments and greenstone implements thus had an 'heirloom' quality that reflected the genealogical transmission of authority and sanctity. Women's fibre products, particularly intricately woven and bordered flax cloaks, were likewise closely associated with the transmission of life, but also marked the inevitable cycle of aging and death through their impermanence.

Greenstone artifacts were not treasures simply because the material was valued, as other stones and precious metals are valued elsewhere: the material was rare and could only be obtained through trade with South Island groups, but possessed ritual and historical significance

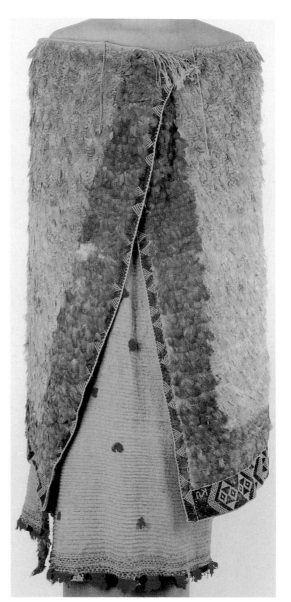

66 (*above*) *Hei-tiki* pendant,
between 1500 and 1800. Ht 4¾ in.

67 (*right*) Feather cape made by
Makurata Paitini, Tuhoe tribe,
c. 1900. 41⅜ × 53½ in.

beyond mere scarcity. In some cases, the greenstone form of a particular artifact type may have encompassed others, in the sense that the effects of the magic worked upon a priest's greenstone fish-hook might extend to the hooks of all men of a tribe. More commonly, objects made of nephrite were significant because they had been handed down over many generations; in some cases, adzes and *hei tiki* were presented as gifts to another group, under special and unusual circumstances, and later returned.

Taonga (Maori treasures) are understood as the inalienable property of the collectivity, or of particular descent lines, but may also be circulated while retaining a permanent association with their original owners. These heirlooms were thus resonant because they embodied genealogies and narratives describing the paths of gifts in the context of wars, alliances and marriages in an object form. The idea that *taonga* may move away from their true owners while remaining essentially attached to them has become increasingly important in recent decades: it is now becoming better understood among white audiences and institutions that Maori art works are not specimens of an ancient material culture, but treasures closely associated with living tribal identities, which retain a *tapu* character and must be appropriately respected if misfortune is to be avoided. Recent exhibitions have therefore been framed by adapted rituals that mark and protect the sanctity of carvings, flax cloaks and other valuables; under indigenous control, these objects have recovered *mana* and prestige that has, for most of the twentieth century, been inadequately recognized in European-controlled museums. Art remains of distinctive importance at a tribal level, but is also a source of pan-Maori political and cultural affirmation in New Zealand, which is defining itself increasingly as a bicultural nation in which indigenous and white settler traditions are both of fundamental importance. This politicization of traditional art is not really the novel development it might appear. Ancestral carvings always embodied presences within a wider field of differences that were once regional or tribal and subsequently 'racial' and ethnic: relations of exchange, alliance and conflict evolved between neighbouring Maori, with white settlers and in the late nineteenth and twentieth centuries on a broader scale, with a dominant white settler society and other migrants, including many Samoans, Tongans and Cook Islanders, who have revived the connection between New Zealand and tropical Polynesia. In these shifting contexts, Maori art forms have consistently been intended to awe visitors and overwhelm them with the prestige and power of their hosts.

CHAPTER THREE

The Art of War

Warfare was of central importance in many Pacific societies, as a vehicle for male prestige, as an appropriation of other groups' life-energies and as a moment in a cycle of creative and destructive exchange. In some areas, fighting had the familiar political and military objectives of securing dominance, seizing land and obtaining slaves or tribute, but it was more typically founded in demands for vengeance, or for sacrificial victims that were essential in rituals such as those that took place when a new men's house or war canoe was inaugurated. Usually, therefore, war proceeded through the capture or assassination of individuals, rather than through large-scale conflict.

Fighting and art are connected in the sense that weapons, canoes, the heads of slain enemies and the bodies of warriors are often decorated. Which objects are elaborated, and in what ways, depends on how fighting is itself conceived and related to other practices. Acts of violence, for instance, may be understood as moments in specific cycles of revenge, perhaps simultaneously as individual and collective accomplishments that transform the status of a renowned warrior and enhance the vigour of his community. Whatever the particular understanding of fighting, art in this context is likely to be part of an experienced process, rather than an 'image' that we might productively understand as part of a system of collective representation. Designs can be said to have belonged to larger cultural systems in the sense that they possessed meanings that expressed wider preoccupations and beliefs, but their expressiveness was highly practical: as I suggest throughout this book, the meanings that Western viewers look for, and take to be integrally important in works of art, are less important than those works' effectiveness. From the viewpoint of a warrior, the visual properties of clubs, spears and shields ideally created terror in the minds of prospective victims, and awe among one's associates.

This is evident especially in the case of Asmat shields and woodcarvings, which have justly aroused great interest outside West Papua since they began to be systematically collected in the early twentieth century, mainly by Dutch colonists, missionaries and ethnographers.

The Asmat lived mainly on sago, in villages of a few hundred, scattered across a vast swampy plain that enticed few intruders. Contact with Europeans was consequently limited until the 1930s, when administrative posts and missions were established, but head-hunting was not effectively suppressed until the early 1960s, around the time when Asmat were first intensively studied by ethnologists. Over this period, also, Indonesia was asserting control over the whole of the western half of New Guinea, initially in a heavy-handed way that saw indigenous ceremonies and art stifled and many old carvings destroyed. Since the early 1970s, international interest, a more culturally liberal attitude on the part of Catholic missionaries and demand on the part of collectors and tourists, has encouraged the revival of Asmat carving, for a regional museum in Agats as well as for export. The forms of Asmat art that have interested outsiders are produced almost exclusively by men. Shields once crucial to both the imagining and the practice of head-hunting may continue to have ceremonial uses, but are now primarily commodities; small-scale versions of traditional ancestor carvings, which appeal to collectors' interests in figurative art, are also now made.

Before Christianity, large men's houses were the focus of ceremonial life, which revolved around mortuary cults, preparations for head-hunting raids and initiation ceremonies. For Asmat, death was invariably caused by enemies, either by magic or by killing, and the souls of the dead were apt to wander unhappily, causing misfortune until they had been avenged. Disposing of the dead was not an immediate matter of burial but a process entailing the representation of the dead in carving, sometimes their revisiting the settlement under ritually controlled circumstances, and head-hunting expeditions that, if successful, revenged them. Ancestors were then supposed to travel away permanently; their vitality would be passed on to the living, particularly through the sago palms that were identified with women and that produced food from within their trunks in a manner that paralleled the growth of babies within women's bodies.

Asmat generally identify trees with human beings, and the fruit specifically with human heads; a number of fruit-eating birds are therefore closely identified with head-hunters and are conspicuous in the iconography of shields and mortuary art. The praying mantis was also of distinctive importance, because it is said to appear wooden yet human in its characteristic movements; and, as is well known, the head of the male is sometimes bitten off by the female while mating. A praying mantis motif in profile is sometimes doubled to depict a

68 (*opposite*) *Bisj* poles, Buepis village, Fajit River, Casuarina Coast, south-west New Guinea.

human being, or reduced to a highly schematized zigzag; seemingly abstract patterns were therefore in fact saturated with allusions to the body and its decapitation.

68   The dead were represented in sculpture, especially in the *bisj* poles that were produced for periodic mortuary ceremonies. The generalized association between trees and human life was expressed more specifically in identifications between tree-felling and life-taking practices. Mangrove trees were cut down, decapitated, skinned and shouted over triumphantly by women as they were brought into the village; then they were fashioned into poles up to five metres high that featured carvings of several dead individuals, and a striking openwork projection from between the legs of the highest figure, referred to as its penis. These *bisj* were not generally preserved permanently, but produced for occasions when a number of poles were lined up, in front of which warriors boasted of their powers and promised to revenge the people represented. (While, incidentally, this might be taken to be a patently martial and patriarchal cultural preoccupation, it is notable that women were supposed to goad men on to fight and take heads; successful and unsuccessful warriorhood was respectively rewarded by women's sexual favours and marked by their denial.) Once vengeance had been accomplished, it was hoped that the spirits would use the canoe-like poles to travel downriver toward the sea and beyond that to the realm of the dead. After the ceremony, the *bisj* were abandoned and left to decompose among sago palms, to which their vigour was ideally transferred. It might be pointed out that in the Sepik, agricultural fertility was similarly believed to depend upon successful head-hunting: it was thought that unless heads were taken, the yams so central to male prestige would simply rot in the ground. Cultural affinities between the two areas appear to have been obscured by the fact that warfare had been suppressed for longer in the Sepik by the time most ethnographers worked in the area.

69   At another Asmat festival (the *jipae*) the recent dead are permitted to revisit briefly the world of the living, in which they appear in ropework and basketwork costumes; the missionary Gerardus Zegwaard suggests that having witnessed the vigour and happiness of their kin, the deceased must be convinced that there is no reason at all why they should not abandon this world definitively, and move on to the realm of the dead. Even if this interpretation presumes too neat a rationale for a ceremony that also conspicuously dramatizes conflict between men and women, it underlines the point that the enduring presence of the dead is a problem, which ritual actions seem to mark and express

69 The mask costumes of the
jipae festival, Amanamkai
village, central Asmat, 1961.

rather than permanently solve. The common idea that tribal religion commemorates ancestors is not at all apt for this case: although certain individuals are indeed commemorated in the naming of shields, the effort as a whole aims not to celebrate the dead or sustain their presence, but to get rid of them.

Heads were required not only for vengeance and reinvigoration, but were also central to initiation rites for young men. Initiates had to take a head, which they would cradle and meditate upon for a few days, absorbing the enemy warrior's power, before undertaking a canoe journey towards the sea, the domain of the dead; in the course of the trip the youth became frailer and frailer, mimicking senility, before being plunged into the sea by an older sponsor, to die and be reborn as a man. Killing was therefore, in manifold ways, a precondition for growth and life.

70 (*above*) Shield, Unir River, north-west Asmat,
collected 1913. Ht 75⅜ in.

71 (*above right*) Shield, made by Tjokotsj,
Atjametsj village, central Asmat, collected 1961.
Ht 65¾ in.

72 (*above*) Shield, carved by Ndaji, Manep village, upper Unir River and Utumbuwe River area, north–west Asmat, collected 1970. Ht 71⅜ in.

73 (*right*) Shield, Woméni village, Suwa River, Citak, collected *c.* 1954. 75⅜ in.

Beside the *bisj* poles, the shield is the most elaborately decorated Asmat artifact, and was probably less important as a material defence against enemy spears than as a psychologically powerful weapon in itself. The shield as a whole was named after an ancestor, and its designs often stood for other dead individuals – not necessarily ancestors, but often an owner's younger brother or sister, whom the warrior would no doubt seek to avenge. Although some shields depict readily recognizable human figures, and some incorporate a face on the top, above a dense field of motifs, figures are often highly stylized, and would be assumed to be abstract, in the absence of information that ethnographers such as Adrian Gerbrands obtained from owners at the time of collection. Shields were initially made for a shield feast, after which warriors would venture off on a head-hunting raid, aiming to avenge those after whom their own shields were named. The owner, rather than the carver, is the individual most profoundly associated with the object, and on his death it is generally broken and interred with the body; this, incidentally, tended to be the case across the Pacific, for weapons and other items of intimate property, such as wooden headrests.

In the northern Asmat region, the shield was not broken, but passed on to the son, who promised to fight as effectively as his father. This seems to mark, in a different way, a fundamental concern in Asmat thought with the absence created by death, which is a kind of deficit requiring both closure through vengeance and the replacement of the dead by the living. Although life flows between tree and human forms, as sago nurtures living people, and the dead are replanted in the form of *bisj* in the forest to regenerate the sago, life is itself irreducible and non-convertible. The idea that the dead can be compensated for with shell valuables and that food or brides can be exchanged for other things, which is important in other Melanesian societies, is here inconceivable. As head-hunting subtracts life from another group, it sustains one's own.

One of the most conspicuous non-human motifs on shields is the flying fox, which, like the birds mentioned earlier, is associated with head-hunting because it bites fruit from trees, which are identified with human heads. Hour-glass and hooked crescent shapes refer to ornaments worn by successful head-hunters, and an S-shape images the cut through which the belly of a crocodile or human victim is opened. The shield is thus replete with references to predation and death, and is known by other warriors to join the vigour of the ancestor after whom it is named to that of the man who bears it now. Shields

70–3

70,72

15

74

Flying fox motif from a shield in the style of the north-west Asmat region.

Flying fox motif from a shield from the north-west Asmat region.

A large human figure from a shield in the style of the central Asmat region.

A praying mantis motif from a shield in the style of the central Asmat region.

74 Asmat motifs

seemed to be intrinsically powerful and were used not only in actual fighting, but otherwise displayed and brandished at certain times in efforts to guard against or scare away evil spirits.

The formal organization of the shields reinforces their aggressive head-hunting iconography. The patterns stand out very powerfully, usually in orange ochre, outlined in black against a white background, 72 and are on the whole symmetrical horizontally and partially symmetrical vertically within the design fields, if not over the whole surface. They are, however, also charged with a sense of movement that arises 73 in part from the curved or interlocking structure of the motifs, and also from a twist or asymmetry often present in the overall shape. Though presumably derived from the original form of the buttress root from which the shield was cut, this imbalance tends to be exaggerated rather than redressed by the disposition of carvings. A sense of action and power arises also from the relation between principal motifs and subordinate elements in some shields, in which individual crescent or hook forms seem the offspring of dominant central humans or flying foxes that are energetically extending and replicating themselves. In the context of fighting, this visual power was of course 70,71 dramatically enhanced, as the shield was seen – perhaps only seen – in rapid and confusing motion. It has even been suggested that the motifs were so terrifying that enemies were not merely alarmed but paralysed by them, that they simply dropped their weapons and scarcely resisted capture. Even if this is not literally the case, it does attest to an ideal of efficacy in the minds of carvers, an ideal indirectly born out by the efforts that warriors would venture into enemy villages to steal shields: unless the objects were taken to possess great power in themselves, this would hardly have been worth the risk.

Head-hunting was also extensively practised in the western Solomon Islands, particularly by the inhabitants of New Georgia and Simbo, who preyed upon those of other islands such as Santa Isabel and Choiseul. Although some fighting was motivated by offences committed by enemy groups, the idea of revenge was not generally significant; heads were required more for the inauguration of new canoes and canoe houses and to release the widows of chiefs from mourning. The positions of powerful men in the Solomons depended very much on their accomplishments: those of great renown were successful organizers of head-hunting and trading expeditions, if not necessarily great warriors themselves. They succeeded in attracting wealth in the form of shell rings, which they deployed in the staging of feasts, supporting dependants, building new houses and canoes and purchasing war captives, who were virtually adopted but nevertheless

75 War Chief of Owa Raha greeting visitors with gifts of shell money, Eastern Solomon Islands, *c.* 1930.

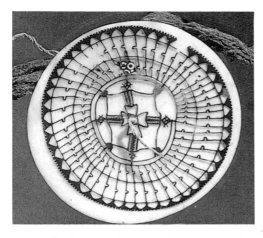

76 *Kapkap*, Solomon Islands. W. 5 in.

compelled to work in gardens or in a kind of ritualized prostitution that enabled their chiefs to accumulate further supplies of shell money.

From the mid-nineteenth century onwards, Europeans traded extensively around New Georgia, particularly for tortoiseshell; chiefly men became more wealthy and head-hunting was intensified. The warriors of the region acquired a reputation for ferocity, but raiding was suppressed not long after the group became a British protectorate in 1893. The administrator, Charles Woodford, had travelled and lived in the region for some time and was aware of the ritual centrality of canoes in the business of head-hunting; he opted for the drastic method of simply destroying many vessels, which evidently did put an end to the practice. The cultural centrality of head-hunting is marked by the fact that after 'pacification', the status of traditional leaders declined dramatically, many ceremonies and the exchange system based around shell valuables were abandoned, art connected with war and feasting declined and missionaries made rapid inroads. The history of New Georgia offers a striking contrast to the Massim region of Papua New Guinea, where the famous *kula* gift-exchange system studied by Malinowski, and the associated art forms, have continued to flourish through the twentieth century, absorbing new categories of valuables and being extended to new areas, including the cities in which exchange-partners now reside. Despite connections in the Massim between warfare and exchange, the vigour of the latter clearly did not depend on the former to the same degree. In the western Solomons, carving for tourists has been revived, but most substantial museum collections only date from the nineteenth century.

89

Shells and shell rings of various kinds were conspicuous in personal ornaments, exchange and ritual in New Georgia and through most of the Solomon Islands. The ornaments included *kapkap*, intricate open-work tortoiseshell patterns occasionally including human or bird figures, which were also produced further west, in New Ireland and the Admiralty Islands. Shell rings of high grades were associated with deities and ancestral power, and were presented at shrines, often to ensure good crops, good fishing or successful head-hunting; others were less sacred and were given to warriors and craftsmen in reward for taking heads or producing certain articles, and also used somewhat more like currency in exchange for pigs, ornaments, foods and various other goods. Although the shell used in shell money is quite different to the nautilus used extensively in the decoration of wooden objects, and although there is little in the rather disappointing ethnographic sources that indicates what significance was attached to the latter, it seems clear that shell was generally associated very strongly with value, and that value was grounded in exchange and predatory activities – fishing and head-hunting – at sea. Large-scale ceremonies either prepared for or celebrated major expeditions, and successful head-hunting or slave-raiding journeys were rewarded by others

77 Exhibition view of Solomon Island canoes, Übersee Museum, Bremen, 1993.

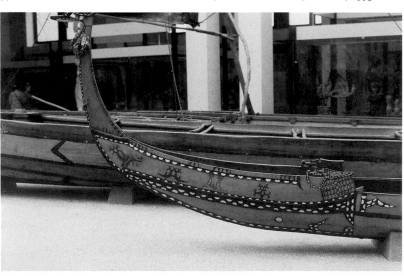

78 Inlaid bowl, Solomon Islands, collected nineteenth century. L. 25 in.

who danced and threw shell valuables onto the sand as a canoe
returned with captives and heads.

The artifacts that figured most directly in feasting were bowls, /8
which were sometimes very large, containing taro and yam-based pud-
dings. These were generally painted black and finely decorated with
pearlshell inlay, mostly with bird and fish motifs. A frigate bird is sometimes attacking or devouring a fish; frigate birds are otherwise
conspicuous in carvings on canoes, weapons, dance clubs and various
ornaments. Frigate birds are large and impressive creatures, but were
specifically important for two reasons: first, they are renowned both
for their aggressive, 'piratical' dispositions, feeding in part by harrying
other seabirds and forcing them to disgorge food and partly because
they frequently travel with schools of bonito. Bonito fishing was highly
valued and a focus of cult activities and initiation in various parts of
the Solomons; many of the rituals associated with blessing and
empowering canoes, and giving thanks to ancestors after successful
journeys, paralleled head-hunting observances, and could even be said
to mimic them. While the frigate bird may not possess any single
meaning, it is not surprising that it figures in tattoos, body-decoration,
feasting utensils and also in canoes, which were of course most directly
connected with predatory maritime activities.

A distinctive feature of the canoe is the prow figureheads. These
painted carvings usually bear striking shell inlay in patterns corresponding with ceremonial face-painting and shell disks in the ears.
One ethnologist reported that the figures frightened away sea demons
who might otherwise imperil the canoe's occupants, which could

conceivably be correct, but possibly only speculation based on assumptions about a magical or animistic 'worldview'. Unlike other forms of human sculpture in the area, which are highly naturalistic, these faces are usually exaggerated and heavily slanted; more impor-

79 tantly, they characteristically hold a head (and in some cases a bird) in their hands. Given that head-hunting was endemic in the western Solomons in the late nineteenth century, it might be presumed that the figureheads, which refer directly to decapitation, were more likely to frighten people than spirits. The reference to killing can be seen to

77 serve the same purpose as the motifs on Asmat shields, but Solomons canoes are less pervaded by the iconography of head-hunting than Asmat art, unless frigate birds really did connote this form of violence more than fishing of a more literal kind.

Aside from the inlaid motifs, which generally consist of schematized frigate birds' wings and more abstract elements, the most distinctive feature of canoe decoration is the Janus-faced figure, often mounted at the top of a high prow, that is itself often heavily adorned with cowrie shells. Janus images, double-headed figures and Siamese twins are remarkably common in Oceanic art, especially in objects associ-ated with chiefly prestige or competitive performance; in the Solomons they also appear in weapons and dance paddles. There is little indigenous exegesis of such images for any area, but this may be because their effect was too obvious to comment upon: a figure that faces both ways can see both ways, and achieves a degree of invulner-ability that anxious head-hunters or frightened villagers must have yearned for.

The content of canoe imagery is not necessarily as important as the sheer display and materialization of value in shell, which is conspicu-ous in much other Solomons art, notably in rare shields decorated with

80 elaborate inlay. The fragility of these pieces has led commentators to suggest that they must have been reserved for ceremonial uses, but it is surely possible that the situation of fighting was precisely the moment at which a powerful man would want to display and project his wealth – bearing in mind that wealth was not a secular value but was recognizable as an expression of magical efficacy and potency. Once again, therefore, an aesthetic of intimidation was in play.

Much that differentiates the Asmat material and the art of the Solomons might be explained through distinct stylistic histories and on the basis of different lifestyles and environments: Asmat had virtu-ally nothing other than wood to work with, while shell is not only abundant around the reefs and lagoons of the Solomons, but it is also

79 Canoe figurehead,
Nguzunguzu, Marovo Lagoon,
New Georgia, Solomon
Islands, collected 1929. Ht 6¾ in.

inevitably present for people who live to a substantial degree from the sea. There is, however, an underlying distinction in kinds of sociality of more fundamental importance. In the Solomons, value and prestige were created and re-created through regional exchange relationships through which many artifacts, raw materials, shell valuables, special foods, heads and captives were obtained. The pattern of production and circulation creates the impression that trade was not undertaken in order to bring goods into areas that did not produce them; rather production seems almost to have been deliberately specialized in order to make the exchange that was an end in itself essential. The reproduction of life and wealth depended not on a 'market' in the sense of commodities, but on relationships through which value was generated, projected and celebrated. Although Asmat engaged in some trade, exchange was in no sense a focus of collective life or individual prestige in a comparable way: ritual focused rather on localized cycles of rebirth and renewal, which required the taking of life; it did not place special value on things that were obtained elsewhere and was wholly devoid of an idea of convertible value, of the kind that might be imaged and celebrated through shell adornment.

It could further be conjectured that shell inlay is appropriate to the art of the Solomons because the powerful contrast between brilliant inlay and wooden background, which is always painted black, exemplifies a kind of contrast intrinsic to the perception of social activities such as feasting and head-hunting. These practices can be seen as expressions of brilliance in themselves, requiring a variety of extraordinary preparations and categorical distinctions from ordinary activities that provide the 'ground' against which predatory accomplishments dazzle. Ritual and ceremonial occasions must always be marked off from conventional routines in a variety of ways; this is a logic of differentiation that appears to be present in the utensils themselves.

In Fiji and western Polynesia, warfare was in no sense devoid of religious significance, but was neither understood in terms of a cycle of killing and fecundity, as was the case among the Asmat, nor imaged in terms of other external relationships, as was the case in the Solomons. Fighting was not restricted to individual killing of the kind associated with ritually motivated head-hunting; it was instead integral to the expansion and contraction of rivalrous chiefdoms. Great emphasis was placed on the prowess and accomplishments of individual warriors, and artistic elaboration was accordingly focused upon the weapons themselves, and especially upon clubs that were ornately carved and stylistically diversified. Some were shaped like short, broad paddles; others broadened gradually from handle to head; others were asymmetrical, terminating in a bulb and lethal point, or a thick triangular projection similar to a gun barrel. 'Rootstock' clubs incorporated the trunk of a small sapling and an irregular head derived from its roots; in other types the heavy end was worked from the join of branch and limb. Decoration was in some cases minimal; certain – mainly Tongan types – were, however, covered in incised geometric patterns that occasionally included figurative elements, such as various animals and men wielding clubs.

The most complex carvings are certainly on the Marquesan clubs known as *u'u*, which have long been regarded by their collectors as

82,83

61

94

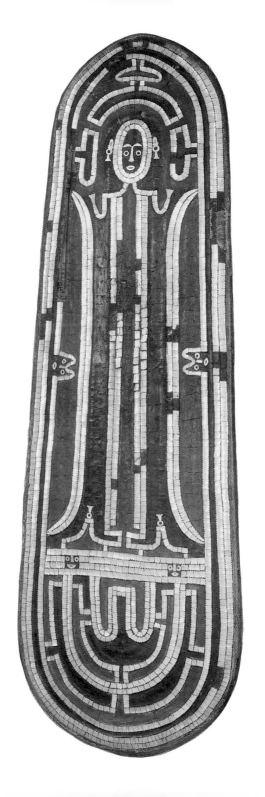

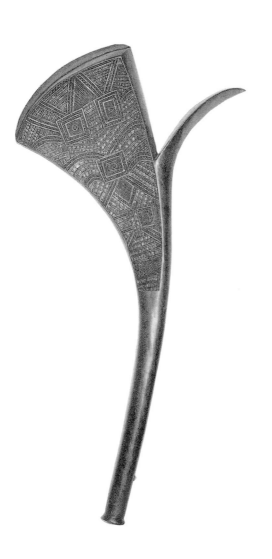

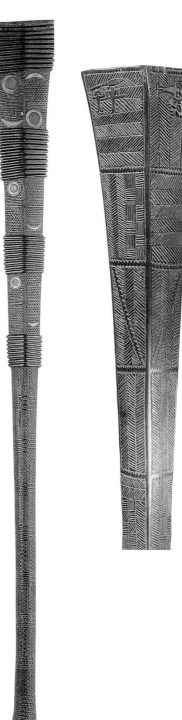

81 (*above*) Lipped club, Fiji. Ht 24⅛ in.

82 (*right*) Club, Tonga. Ht 43¾ in.

83 (*far right*) Detail of coconut-stalk club, Tonga, collected *c.* 1824. Ht 36¼ in.

especially fine expressions of Polynesian sculpture. The head takes the form of a flattened double-sided face, with prominent eyes marked out in radiating grooves; but additional smaller faces constitute these eyes' pupils, nose, forehead and often also the edges of the main faces, which are transformed into the profiles of subsidiary faces. Beneath the lugs that mark off this main face is a field of curving, but basically quadrangular design, resembling Marquesan tattoo motifs that are also used on wooden bowls among other objects, and this field frequently incorporates at least one further pair of eyes. Given that a club of this type might feature some fourteen faces, the effort of multiplication might be thought somehow to empower the weapon's bearer; such speculation, I suggest in the next chapter, is supported by the proliferation of faces in tattoo designs, which were certainly intended to reinforce the warrior's body. 81

These very heavy hardwood weapons certainly had awful effects, but their intricate carving was directed as much at display and performance as actual fighting; the point that war dances, self-decoration and sham fights could absorb more energy than conflict with the enemy is something of a commonplace in European accounts. For those observers, the implication was that these barbarians were vain; but in most other societies military display has surely involved a similar kind of congratulatory self-knowledge.

While fighting entailed performance virtually everywhere, the theatricality of war and the attendant art forms assumed what could be seen as different modalities, according to the ways in which killing was associated with the regeneration of the collectivity, imaged in terms of other practices and actually carried out. In the present, when art is understood generally as a benign and enriching form of collective self-expression, it is valuable to recall that these objects were not emblems of some tribal or ethnic identity – not images that permitted some kind of social cohesion, but weapons that figured effectively in a defiant, highly aestheticized terrorism.

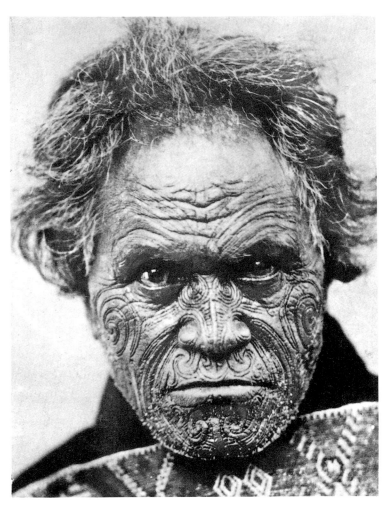

84 Tomika Te Mutu, nineteenth-century Maori chief.

CHAPTER FOUR

The Art of the Body

In the late eighteenth century, tattooing was widely practised in eastern Oceania. In the Marquesas, the whole body was tattooed in spectacular fashion; equally striking were the Maori, who employed a deep chiselling technique to produce elaborate curvilinear full-face designs on men and chin tattoos on women. In western Polynesia, Samoan men were densely tattooed around the buttocks and thighs, a custom emulated in Tonga and reversed in Fiji, where women, rather than men, bore such markings. In Tahiti, both men and women wore arched tattoos around the buttocks and thighs, and might also carry diverse star and circle motifs around the chest and arms.

87,91
88
85

86

The latter fascinated early European visitors, who were otherwise entranced by Tahitian society and sexuality, and a few officers and many common sailors, including most of the notorious *Bounty* mutineers, obtained tattoos on Tahiti or elsewhere in the South Seas in the late eighteenth and early nineteenth centuries. Although tattooing was practised in other parts of the world, this was the beginning of the fashion among British seamen that subsequently spread among

95

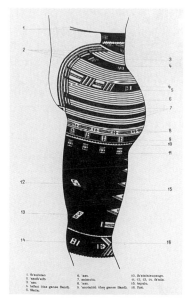

85 (*left*) Nineteenth-century Samoan male tattoo, from Carl Marquardt, *Die Tätowirung beider Geschlecter in Samoa*, 1899.

86 (*above*) Tahitian tattoos sketched by Sydney Parkinson in 1769, during Cook's first voyage.

88 Portrait of a New Zealand man with tattoos, by Sydney Parkinson, 1773. 15¼ × 11⅜ in.

87 Paetini, chiefly woman of Taiohae, Nukuhiva, northern Marquesas Islands, 1838.

marginalized underclasses within Europe. The word tattoo is, like taboo, in a small but culturally significant group of European words derived from Polynesian languages, the original term being *tatau* in both Samoan and Tahitian. The etymology reminds us that cross-cultural borrowing in the Pacific was not a one-way process through which islanders emulated the 'more advanced' European cultures, but one through which Polynesian self-decoration also had a considerable impact on the culture of the body in the West and beyond. Moreover, the connection points to residual affinities between Tahitian tattooing and subcultural tattooing in the West – despite the pronounced cultural differences – especially since these traditions have converged again in contemporary tattooing among Maori urban gangs and Samoans in New Zealand.

Early observers frequently assumed that tattooing was an emblem of rank, a view that was seemingly substantiated by the fact that some persons of chiefly status were heavily tattooed. In a number of key

89

ÎLES SANDWICH. UN OFFICIER DU ROI EN GRAND COSTUME.

89 Chief or chiefly attendant with tattoos, Sandwich Islands, *c.* 1819.

instances, however, persons of the very highest rank were not tattooed, and in those cases where men are tattooed and women not, or vice versa, it is arguable that the untattooed sex possessed greater rank or sanctity. Understandably enough, European writers frequently equated ranked Oceanic societies with the patriarchal and feudal polities of early and medieval Europe. What is problematic is not the assumption that there may have been affinities, but the fact that European political forms were themselves understood so simplistically. Power is almost always ambiguous; where political relationships are created at once through aggression and conquest, and through status and sanctity, there will inevitably be tensions between aspects of power that are uneasily combined in one person and ruling title, or explicitly differentiated between those occupying martial and sacred chieftainships. Commonly, installation rituals seek to incorporate and domesticate transgressive powers, but this is not to say that such rites in fact effectively produce a happy political synthesis.

The practice of tattooing, which involves violence to the body, did not simply 'express' political ambiguities, but was arguably central to their constitution. This is suggested simply by the fact that tattooing was not just a painful and protracted operation, but a kind of penetrative violence: a narrow comb-like bone instrument that had been dipped into the colouring agent was rapidly hammered into the skin, moved and hammered again, creating a dense field of stained punctures. As if this were unlikely to be sufficiently excruciating at the best of times, people in a number of areas attached particular importance to the tattooing of especially sensitive areas such as the tongue, penis, labia and eyelids. I do not suggest that there are direct parallels between the constellation of desire around the scene of tattooing and sadomasochistic practices elsewhere, but it is clear that if the bearing and baring of tattoos paraded an accomplishment, their acquisition nevertheless demanded subjection to those elders or chiefs who compelled or sponsored the operation. Though initiation was not formalized in Polynesia in the way it was in much of New Guinea, the ordeal of tattooing has much in common with the beatings, circumcision and nose-piercing that are often important within initiation cycles. Such practices are usually painful, but are understood to harden the body; with the addition of grease, paint and other decorations, they also typically render it brilliant and attractive, while signifying maturity or a particular phase of adolescence. The effort to reinforce the body, and this ambiguity of degradation and empowerment, is symptomatic of the effect of body art in Oceania.

90 Tattooing in Samoa, late nineteenth century.

In addition to associating tattooing with rank, European observers frequently noted that untattooed men, especially in Samoa, Tonga and the Marquesas, were denied women's sexual favours and generally treated with contempt. In a number of memoirs, European men who 'went native' in the early nineteenth century claimed that in order to form relationships with local women, and to conform otherwise, they were obliged to acquire tattoos. There is no doubt that, in general, Polynesians and visiting Europeans took a person's sexual attractiveness to be enhanced by tattooing; this does not, however, explain the practice, and certainly does not explain why it should be greatly elaborated in some Polynesian societies and much diminished in others. Tattooing was indeed closely connected with sexuality, but (as with political status) not because adornment was valued in a straightforward way.

Tattooing, as a practice that altered the skin, or that could be seen to add an artificial skin, was understood as an important reinforcement of the body, a stage as vital as other moments in the life cycle, such as birth and death. Its importance in these terms was not separate from its political significance; rather, notions of evolving sanctity, vulnerability, armament and what can be called 'deconception' –

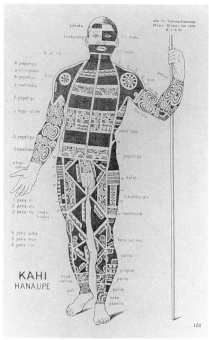

91 Fully tattooed Marquesan man, engraving after a drawing made in 1804.

92 Male tattoo designs, Marquesas Islands, from Karl von den Steinen, *Die Marquesaner und ihrer Kunst*, 1925–8.

93 (*opposite*) Carved arm with tattoo designs, Marquesas Islands, thought to be a stand for offerings, collected by Robert Louis Stevenson, *c.* 1890–4, Ht 24 in.

the disaggregation of bodily elements at the time of death – were themselves linked with political relationships and the re-creation of those relationships over generations.

The most striking feature of Marquesan tattooing is the sheer multiplication and density of designs. Marquesan men were, for the most part, warriors, and the elaboration can be read along the lines suggested in the previous chapter for Asmat shields: given the movement of the body, and the structured yet unstable organization of motifs, the warrior invests himself with a form of visual armour that distracts and ideally disorients his opponents. Given that a competitive warrior ethos was more accentuated in the disorderly and conflict-ridden Marquesas than the comparatively more stable societies of

92

104

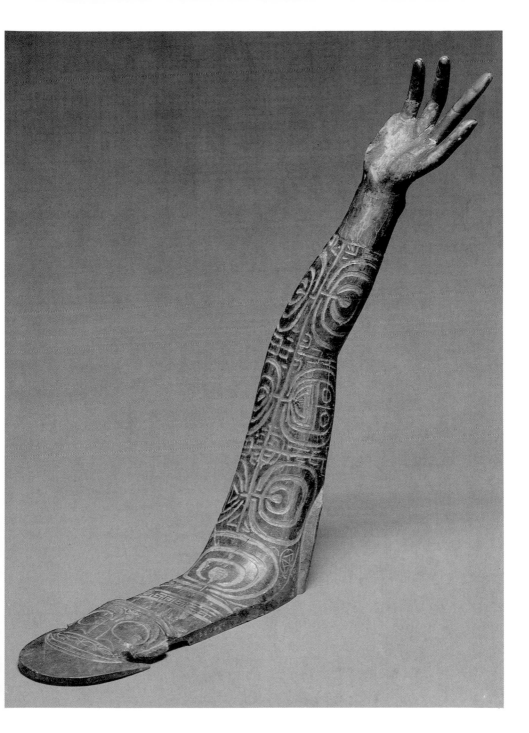

Tahiti, Tonga and Mangareva, it might consequently be expected that Marquesan tattooing would be more elaborate.

But this is only part of the story. In order to have a fuller sense of the efficacy of Marquesan tattooing, a detour into Polynesian ideas of the person and the body is called for. The Western idea of the individual as a self-subsistent agent – that is, immature as a child but nevertheless complete – is alien to Oceanic ideas that see the person as a *divisible* entity incorporating substances and attributes from a number of sources. This may be so in a corporeal sense: bones are considered a hardened form of the father's semen and the blood a direct inheritance from the mother. In a social, rather than a physiological sense, however, various capacities and attributes of the person are seen to be bestowed through gifts or nurture, as they can be made equally visible, extended or disposed of through exchange relations. Just as the person is not complete at birth, but produced through a variety of subsequent transformations, including initiation, defloration and marriage, death does not definitively undo what has been put together. In the Asmat case, it has been shown that a person does not depart for the land of the dead until he or she has been avenged; in other societies, mortuary gifts to kin and those related by marriage may repay or undo the bundle of debts of substance and nurture that the deceased embodied. Operations upon the actual corpse, such as the separation of bones and flesh, and a secondary burial of the former, frequently have the similar effect of separating the multiple elements that are drawn together in conception, birth and subsequent gifts of nurture, land and ritual knowledge.

In the Polynesian case, the notions that are most salient to the life cycle and tattooing arise from a highly dualistic worldview in which the realm of darkness, death and the gods (the *po*) is juxtaposed with the world of the living and light (the *ao* or *te ao marama*). This is understood as a matter of cosmogonic sequence, in the sense that an epoch of darkness predated the emergence of light, but also as a matter of enduring coexistence. The *po* is the source not only of divine influence, but also of fertility, children and general efficacy. Agricultural growth, successful fishing and many forms of specialized work ranging from tattooing to house-building required sacrifices to deities which would ensure their presence or favour; chants at the beginning of such activities summoned the deities from the world of darkness, while those at their conclusion sought to compel the gods to return. This auspicious presence – desirable temporarily rather than permanently – rendered activities, places and objects *tapu*, a condition of heightened sanctity that differed categorically from the ordinary condition of things in a world prone to dissipation, to the peril of the work or growth in question, and contagiously threatening to non-*tapu* persons or objects in the vicinity. *Tapu* thus required delicate management. It had to be protected for the duration of a task, such as canoe-building or planting, but subsequently had to be lifted, so that the object or product could enter into common use. Without controlled *tapu* removal, people other than the specialists directly engaged in an activity were liable to be fatally afflicted, and virtually all malaise was attributed to *tapu* violation, where it was not taken to result from sorcery.

The newborn emerge directly from the *po* and are thus intensely and threateningly *tapu*; they therefore underwent rites that diminished their *tapu* character and made intercourse between themselves and others (and specifically their parents) safe. In Tahiti, where beliefs were broadly similar to those in the Marquesas, this was effected by a blood-letting and mixing procedure: the child's blood was joined with that of less sacred people, and thereby rendered less contagious. This was not a one-off rite but an operation that was performed a number of times through childhood, presumably because sanctity was too intense to be removed entirely on a single occasion. Until the whole sequence of rites had been effected, the child remained threatening to the parents in various ways, and could not eat with them or touch their food, without rendering it *tapu* or highly dangerous to them. Desanctifying procedures were, moreover, of localized and contextual effect. People, and especially those of chiefly status, and men in relation to women, carried even into maturity a kind of personal *tapu* that could be diminished, or reabsorbed into the world of gods and darkness. This was liable to take place if they were placed beneath, or in inappropriate proximity to a less *tapu* thing or person, and especially to a bodily orifice such as the vagina, which was considered the most significant and active channel of movement between the worlds of darkness and light. Bodies, in short, were dangerously unstable, prone to threaten others, and to be threatened.

Tattooing appears to have partially redressed this problematic permeability. The operation wounded the skin under controlled circumstances and then fixed and sealed its surfaces with motifs such as additional faces. As vision and power were closely identified, a proliferation of eyes conveyed diminished vulnerability. The process of wrapping in images – to take the Marquesan term that Alfred Gell has suggested expresses the essence of tattooing – not only provided the warrior with an additional skin or shell, but diminished both the body's proneness to contagion and its capacity to suffer through attracting and diminishing the *tapu* of others. In Tahiti, accordingly, a small, easily visible tattoo on the arm marked the completion of the sequence of desanctifying rituals just alluded to, and the non-contagious character of the person.

In the Marquesas, the reinforcing character of tattooing is suggested by the designs, in which turtles and anthropomorphic motifs are conspicuous. Turtles were occasionally substituted for humans in sacrifices, a distinctive status that might be attributed to their amphibious ambiguity; their travel between land and sea may also possibly have suggested the movement of the dead, who reached the afterworld via the sea. The particular appropriateness of turtles in tattooing iconography must moreover be accentuated by the affinity between their armour and the 'shells' and protective skins that tattooing ideally provided.

The anthropomorphic images are highly reduced and schematized, perhaps precisely to facilitate their multiplication: a plethora of additional bodies could be seen to empower proportionately the otherwise weak individual. The same idea may be present in Tahitian buttock tattoos, if their arches and circular forms are schematized forms of the sculpted faces of carved deities. While the motifs cannot definitely be identified in these terms, the resulting doubling of faces back-to-back resonates with the Janus forms conspicuous in Tahitian carving, notably in the ornamental fly-whisks of chiefs. The wider prevalence of Janus imagery in Oceanic art has already been alluded to; Gell has persuasively argued that the doubling of the face, in particular, expresses an omnipotence and invulnerability that people such as warriors and chiefs were driven toward. (It might be noted in this context that one of the most common methods of assassination was a stealthy club on the back of the head, which an additional pair of eyes would indeed preclude.) Spells referring to preparations for war were chanted as the tattooing was conducted, and can be seen to take physical effect in the skin, to fix themselves, through the process of perforation and healing.

This consolidation of protective skins also recapitulated the constitution of ancestral deities such as Ta'aroa, who are said to be born as shapeless miscarriages or clots of blood, but who successively acquire skins relating to different strengths and personal attributes. In Samoa, the final tattoo element to be applied to the body covered the navel; this can be seen to consummate the closure or armature of the body, and replaces the physical trace of natural birth. This

94,126

94 Anthropomorphic figure with two heads, Tahiti, Society Islands,
collected 1822. Ht 23 in.

'overwriting' of the connection with the mother by patriarchal artifice is characteristic of male initiation elsewhere in Oceania (among both Sepik and Asmat peoples, for instance, discussed in previous chapters), though contrasting and mutually appropriated male and female powers were not a focus of cultural preoccupation in eastern Polynesia. The operation of reinscription seems again in this case self-defeating, given that the effort to cover the warrior's origin in the mother's body only draws attention to what is only notionally concealed. This suggests that tattooing did not bring about a consummate or effective recomposition of the body, but exhibited its profoundly ambiguous character.

The place of tattooing in the life cycle is further attested to by the remarkable Marquesan practice of removing the skin on death. Marquesans believed in an afterworld divided into a gloomy realm occupied by former servants and common people, and a paradisiacal domain presided over by the goddess Oupu, into which the spirits of chiefs and other persons of rank might be admitted. Oupu, however, was disgusted by tattooing, and certain ferocious deities were said to wait for the dead at the entrance to the afterworld, ready to tear to pieces anyone who arrived with any trace of it. Consequently, the wife or relatives of a tattooed individual were obliged painstakingly to rub away the corpse's skin, and all tattooing with it, over a period of months, after which the body was placed in a sacred ground, from which the spirit was later understood to depart by canoe to the underworld.

This was to reverse the process of birth and growth. As the individual emerged at birth in an excessively *tapu* state from the *po*, and had to be deconsecrated, protected and rendered both less contagious and less vulnerable, the person moving out of the world of light and life and back into the world of night had their wrappings removed and their sanctity enhanced, such that they might be assimilated again to their prior condition. Just as men created a person in the world through the addition of artificial skins, women created a person for the next world by undoing those skins, by stripping away the armour through which the warrior had been constructed. This is consistent with the fact that certain sacred chiefs of the highest rank were not tattooed. These individuals were not powerful and renowned because they staged feasts and conquered their neighbours, but because they possessed a kind of encompassing sanctity that arose from close genealogical connections with founding deities, which produced generalized prosperity. This kind of sacredness would have been

95 The beachcomber John Rutherford, with a facial tattoo obtained in New Zealand and chest tattoos done in the Society Islands and possibly Rotuma.

compromised by precisely the insulation and deconsecration that a warrior's aggression and transgression required. But a warrior was deconsecrated for a certain phase of worldly existence, rather than permanently. Accordingly, as Gell has persuasively argued, his tattooing had to be removed in order that he might recover the absolute, disembodied sacredness that characterized immortality in the other world. Tattooing was thus not only an expression or mark of the transgressive mode of Polynesian power, but also an essential element of its making and unmaking.

A peculiar and distinctive feature of religion in Tahiti was a shift, apparently underway at the time of early contact, that saw a traditional sacrifice based around Ta'aroa and closely associated with the ruling chiefs, give way to a cult of the god 'Oro, which had spread from the leeward Society Islands, Raiatea and Borabora (see a further discussion in Chapter 7). 'Oro was worshipped particularly by members of the Arioi society, which, like its counterpart, the Ka'ioi in the Marquesas, provided an alternative life-path for young aristocrats, who would travel extensively through the islands, and were renowned for promiscuity, feasting and theatrical performances. The Arioi were especially notorious in evangelical accounts for infanticide: members of the society were not permitted to reproduce, and at some level the whole institution can be seen as a tactic of high-ranking kin groups that restricted their fertility and therefore the dilution of their status by creating a privileged but non-reproducing subculture.

Arioi had an ambiguous relationship to the central chieftainship in the sense that much of their self-decoration amounted to a 'burlesque imitation' of paramount chiefly insignia; elite Arioi bore full, black leg tattoos and were entitled to wear red cloth, resembling the red feather girdles of the high chiefs that were directly identified with their titular status, and with feathers that originally covered 'Oro's body. There is a good deal of confusion in sources around the nature of the Arioi, which to some degree reflects actual social ambiguities characterizing their position. They indeed behaved transgressively and could comment critically and satirically upon high chiefs through their dramatic performances, but they played an oppositional role more than they really acted oppositionally; in fact, they were intimately connected to the paramount chiefs, who presided over admissions to higher Arioi rank grades, and they played crucial ritual roles themselves during the paramounts' installation ceremonies. Gell has suggested that the density of their tattooing, together with their broader social position as displaced, transgressive aristocrats, suggests

96 Samoan tattooing in Auckland, New Zealand, 1982. The seated man is the tattooing master, Su'a Suluape Petelo; the tattooed man, standing next to his wife, is Sogaimiti Faiga Mamea.

97 Vicki Te Amo, one of many Maori people now reviving traditional tattoos, 1993.

that they exemplified, in a more intensified form, the broader Society Islands practice of reducing contagious sanctity in order to act freely: heavier tattooing reinforced the armour of the body and rendered the observance of personal taboos unnecessary or less necessary. This empowerment, for all its liberty and apparent defiance of chiefly power, ultimately served the cultivation of prestige and was contained within higher chiefly sovereignty.

Tattooing was widely proscribed by missionaries and abandoned in the late nineteenth and early twentieth centuries. In some areas, such as Fiji, where women were tattooed in a fashion that is now interpreted as a particular enhancement of sexuality, revival in the near future is most unlikely while the church remains strong, but tattooing is elsewhere seen more as an expression of cultural pride that attests to roots in tradition, and is accordingly being revived.

Samoan tattooing was never abandoned and is now practised among Samoan migrants in New Zealand, the United States and probably elsewhere. While there are certainly continuities between nineteenth-century meanings and those of the present, these have been incorporated within feelings of ethnic pride, especially important for diasporic Samoans. Accordingly, the designs are now taken to represent core

Samoan values, such as mutual care on the part of an extended family; the canoe and the flying fox, reputed to care for her extended family beneath her wings, are therefore important. Lines refer to genealogies, adventures and accomplishments. As Sulu'ape Paulo II, a prominent Samoan tattoo artist in New Zealand, writes, the 'aso faaifo (curved lines) 'encircle your being as a person of rank, having understood your commitment to incorporate your mother's and father's families into your life. Samoan custom requires men to live entirely for their sisters.' This is not at all untrue to traditional Samoan culture, but it does give tattooing a new value as a bearer of that culture, understood as a total entity. In this new situation also, the bodily marks of women, which were not previously categorized as tattooing, are increasingly being seen in the same terms. Samoans still suffer excruciating pain, conforming with the old duality of subjection and empowerment, although the latter has been transformed to include a claim about distinctiveness in multicultural societies.

In New Zealand, Maori gangs became especially significant in the 1970s, and embodied a disorderly and threatening kind of urban indigenous cultural renaissance that the dominant society found hard to cope with. Their tattoos, frequently done in prison, drew on black power and bikie motifs, but were also loosely influenced by the lines of facial *moko*, in many cases angering Maori with more traditional and politically mainstream inclinations, who objected that the tattoos were done improperly and *tapu* restrictions flouted. Interviewed gang members generally find it difficult to articulate their justifications for the practice, but insist that the tattoos stand for who they are and how they present themselves. Beyond these subcultures, a reinvigorated Maori culture has grown and diversified, and *moko* in a more traditional style are being revived, though produced with an electric needle rather than the traditional chisel. In the case of men, these are often done around the buttocks and thighs rather than on the face, therefore functioning, like Samoan tattooing and the hidden tattoos of the old European aristocracy, as a partially private sign that need not compromise respectable appearances in high-status occupations. It is hard to avoid the view that, despite their slipshod unruliness and the Western origin of many designs, gang tattooing conforms more closely to the practice's earlier logic – in armouring the body and creating awe and fear among beholders.

CHAPTER FIVE

Maternal Symbolism and Male Cults

Women's art forms in the Pacific have been neglected for several reasons. Collectors and curators have taken them to be less visually spectacular than men's products, such as carved ancestor figures; they are readily classified as utilitarian craft items rather than as art; and, often, being made of cloth or fibre, they are difficult to conserve and present problems of display that carving in wood and stone does not. Since Oceanic art began to be described, collected and displayed, therefore, a one-sided understanding emerged, which was consistent with stereotypes of warrior societies and ancestral cults: the conspicuous objects were clubs, spears, masks and effigies. Because Melanesian societies were imaged in masculine and patriarchal terms by nineteenth- and early twentieth-century travellers and missionary writers, and thought to be dominated by elders, witch-doctors and head-hunters, this marginality of women's art is unsurprising.

Although the perception of gender relations in Polynesia had been more positive since the Cook voyages, the idea that women there possessed 'higher' status rested upon ethnocentric criteria, and was based more on the attractiveness of the women from the perspective of male European explorers than any sense of women's own perception of their agency and value. However, in the first half of the twentieth century, a more nuanced understanding of western Pacific societies emerged with the studies of Malinowski, Fortune, Mead and Bateson, some of which were concerned particularly with 'sex roles'. It became evident that male dominance was accentuated in some regions while sexual equality or female dominance might be encountered in others. Terms such as 'equality', however, remained unexamined, and the implications for material culture and art were not explored until much later, when feminist anthropologists initiated a reappraisal of gender relations in Oceanic societies from the 1970s on. It became apparent that even in societies in which male dominance was conspicuous, women's informal power might be considerable, particularly within domains of activity that women themselves valued. So far as art was concerned, even where the most prestigious and sacred objects were produced by men for male cults, a distinct sphere of women's material wealth and exchange might be identified, which earlier observers had overlooked. Annette Weiner, in particular, pointed to the importance of fibre products such as barkcloth, banana-leaf bundles, mats, baskets and flax cloaks that were variously regarded as exchange valuables and heirlooms in many Oceanic societies.

The idea that a definite body of 'women's art' has been neglected is, however, problematic. The work produced by women is not necessarily identified and valued as the work *of* women; its meanings are not necessarily first and foremost grounded in ideas of femininity or in women's reproductive roles. The problem lies in the limited applicability of Western notions of the individual, production and property in Oceania. In European thought it is broadly assumed that the person is a definite and indivisible agent and the producer of particular values, objects and art forms. Melanesian people may certainly, in some contexts, claim their products as their property, and recognize themselves in their actions, but they differ from people elsewhere, and from Europeans in particular, in understanding relationships between producers and products in multiple and divisible terms rather than on a one-to-one basis.

The person is less like the individual in Western ideas than a composite: of maternal and paternal substances, of relations of debt and of ancestral or divine presences. Accordingly, work of any consequential kind, whether it be gardening or weaving, is not understood as an immediate and complete physical process, but as a practice in which relationships with kin, affines, ancestors and others may be acknowledged or marked. Given that so much cult life in Melanesia is energized by sexual difference, and in the Highlands turns particularly upon male mimicry of female procreative power, it is not surprising that forms of work and art forms that are primarily associated with one sex often bear certain attributes of the other. Ideas of both women's and men's art may therefore be inappropriate. Any more elaborate product or object, such as a pig, a house, a garden, a feast, a mask, or a decorated person that emerges from complex relationships and several phases of work, is unlikely to be identified exclusively with one producer or one sex.

In fact, many artifacts that are identified as male or female products are not produced entirely by one sex, but incorporate both male and female contributions: men may for instance gather the pandanus, which women then process and weave into mats, or women's menstrual blood may be incorporated into the paint on masks or other

98 The Telefol women achieve this textured effect with the wide range of shades naturally available from the *Ficus* species.

objects which seem quintessentially male. Much more commonly, men decorate objects which women have produced (this is widely true of pottery in New Guinea, as well as the string bags discussed in this chapter). It should not be assumed either that male elaboration suppresses the female contribution, or that equal contributions are automatically recognized. Rather the operations of covering and superimposition may be ambiguously hierarchical: if the female element is at the core or base of the male, that which is subordinated in one sense appears to be privileged in another.

The string bag, or *bilum* in Melanesian pidgin, is now used all over Papua New Guinea, but was originally produced and used mainly in non-Austronesian-speaking areas – that is, on the New Guinea mainland, excluding certain coastal areas, particularly in the south-east. Bilums are produced through a distinctive looping technique that differs from weaving or knotting in the looseness and flexibility of the product; consequently, they can be employed to carry or contain diverse objects, including garden produce, firewood, arrows, betel nut, personal property and school books; they are also used to carry babies

99 The bast fibres from a mountain *Ficus* species will be beaten, washed and shredded to make spinning string.

and provide a hammock-like cradle. Bags are also exchange items, elements of ceremonial clothing and bearers of ancestral power.

In the Telefol area, on which Maureen MacKenzie focused in a ground-breaking study of the cultural value of bilums, there are many types of bags, ranging from large, expandable all-purpose bilums for women that are a basic item of domestic equipment, to a variety of smaller 'amulet' bilums constructed in a tighter fashion and containing charms or pieces of an ancestor's or warrior's bones. Others mark a woman's condition of mourning, and a special class is decorated with feathers and worn by male initiates of various grades.

98,99   The raw materials are simply plant fibres (mostly *Ficus*), or more recently, imported wool and nylon, together with a pandanus or plastic strip around which in some areas loops are constructed to ensure a standard-sized loop. The tighter, small bilums are worked with a bone or steel needle. The best fibres were not available in all environments and were circulated through trade before European contact; this exchange has become commercialized, and unprocessed or partially processed inner bark is transported around the Highlands by plane and sold at markets. Although bilums are made individually rather than co-operatively, women often loop in casual groups and fit in the preparation of string and actual looping at any available time between other tasks. Children pick up basic spinning techniques and as girls mature they acquire first a basic competence in standard women's bilums and subsequently, to a varying degree, an aptitude in more specialized looping techniques that enable them to make other kinds of bags and produce more aesthetically effective textures and patterns. Older women pass on their knowledge progressively, as younger women acquire competence and responsibility. Bilum-making is thus closely integrated with the flow of female life and sociality.

In other respects women and bilums are closely identified: a bilum is a standard element of female attire, and a finely produced bilum exhibits a woman's productive capacities, as well as often containing the results of her work and fecundity. The fact that the bilum is frequently used as a cradle makes its identification with the woman's body, and specifically her womb, unsurprising: its capacity to expand, and its bulging postition on her back makes for obvious visual affinities between the full bilum and the pregnant body. These identifications become particularly significant at the time of death. All dead were exposed on mortuary platforms in gardens, but individuals of renown were transformed into ancestors. The ritual work was done by a specialist, who 'harvested' the bones after the flesh had decomposed, and placed them inside a prepared bilum; they were then carried as part of a procession to the men's house, hung up and propitiated through pig sacrifices. The way in which the specialist cradled the 100

100 Two women with bilums, 1982. The shape of these net bags, in which they carry produce or a nestling child, echoes the belly of a pregnant woman.

bones and spirit within the bilum mimics the treatment of a baby, and an ordinary loose bag was preferred for this purpose to a sacred amulet bilum on the grounds that the spirit can see and remain comfortable. The contents of these sacred bilums were notionally – but only notionally – secret from women, and in Telefolip village itself, the cult centre for Telefolmin people, these bearers of ancestors' bones are kept both within the men's house and within houses that were exclusively for women.

The significance of bilums as ancestral containers and sacred objects marks the way in which the form can be at once closely identified with womanhood and with ritual powers that sustain both men and women. The form lends itself to extension and elaboration in part because the connections between artifact and woman are themselves pregnant. The meanings of women's art forms are not the same everywhere, and cannot necessarily be derived from women's bodies, because the meanings of the term 'woman' itself are not stable across the Pacific or within New Guinea. In some areas, the woman's role as sister is crucial; or rather, the tension between sisterhood and wifehood, and consequently the conflict between the claims of a woman's brothers and those of her husband and his kin are socially fundamental. Elsewhere, her productivity and procreativity may be emphasized.

Even where a woman is understood above all as a mother, however, 'motherhood' does not possess a constant meaning and value. In the Telefol case, as MacKenzie has shown, the beliefs and myths concerning the ancestral mother-creator, Afek, are of fundamental importance. For related Mountain Ok peoples, as well as Telefolmin, Afek is the source of all nurture and substance, the founder of the sexual division of space and work, and the originator of particular cult houses that she established in the course of movements across the landscape, which are mythologically recounted. Afek is understood to have brought or created everything important in Telefol life, including the staple food, taro, shell valuables and other cult items. These are believed either to have fallen from the bilum that Afek carried, or to be transformations of her menstrual and vaginal secretions. Consequently, the maternal associations of string bags do not simply stand for the maternal capacities of the women who make and carry them today, but they instead resonate with Afek's constitutive and original maternity, which living women and their bilums partake of and recapitulate.

There is a public or secular myth that accounts for the distinct male and female spheres in Telefol society. Afek originally lived in the cult

120

101 Men's feathered bilums express their masculinity and mark the stage of initiation reached.

house and was decorated like a man, while her brother and husband, Umoim, cared for the children and pigs. He did not, however, look after them properly, and they were continually squealing and crying, so Afek reversed the arrangement. She was able to keep the pigs and children content, and was pleased with Umoim's decorated appearance, so decided that from then on women would stay in the women's or family house while men would occupy the cult house. Another version of this myth is acquired only in the course of initiation, and reveals how Afek first exposed and treated Umoim's body and created the first sacred bilum that contained the bones of the dead. Myths of this kind are ritual charters that define and empower male cult practices while situating female powers and origins at their centre.

It is in this context that elaborated bilums are significant. Unlike women's looping, which is engaged in openly and informally, bird feather bilums for initiation ceremonies are made in seclusion by male specialists belonging to particular cult groups, on the basis of a bilum made by the initiate's mother. Usually a man presents his wife with

101

prepared fibres out of which she loops a fine bilum for him to work on. Feathers are collected from hornbills, brush turkeys, eagles and other birds, depending on which initiation level their son is approaching and which bilum is therefore being made. Once feathers are acquired, the quills are cut and looped through the bilum fabric, forming dense but finely shaped rows of feathers that completely cover the looped string base. While these bilums are worn openly by initiated men and connote maleness in the same way that unelaborated bilums connote femaleness, they have more esoteric uses and meanings in ritual activities. In part, the importance of these sacred practices arises simply from the fact that they are secret and exclusive: as in the Sepik, male maturity is dramatized and differentiated from ordinary familial life. But there is more to the esoteric knowledge than sheer mystification.

In the course of initiation, boys are given secret objects, including bamboo tubes of pig fat and face paint, along with information concerning the origin and significance of these things, which are subsequently concealed within the feather bilum. A cucumber – a sign of male, phallic powers – is broken over the initiate at an early point in the ritual, and subsequently incorporated into the bilum with the fat and face paint. Red and white – female and male elements – are thus joined in a process that mimics conception. In a later stage of the initiation ritual, the maturing adolescents are elaborately decorated and reintroduced to the world of women; the women's excitement recapitulates Afek's original pleasure in the spectacle of the decorated Umoim.

As MacKenzie points out in an insightful interpretation of the whole process, the successive phases of the ritual entail a reorientation of self-construction that amounts to a sleight of hand on the part of elders. In the initial stage, the emphasis is upon introducing objects and attendant knowledge enclosed within the bilum, which enables male growth and self-sufficiency. At the later stage, however, display takes the place of concealment, and ripe cucumbers, which are intended to attract women, are brought forth in place of the decaying cucumbers hidden in the bags. Initiates eventually learn that the paint with which they are decorated is not merely derived originally from Afek's nurturant blood, but contains the menstrual blood of living women, considered to be essential to its efficacy. Initially, therefore, a superior form of male procreation, mimicking and refining women's natural creativity, is projected and only partially understood by new initiates; subsequently, the emphasis is upon the underlying comple-

102 A young Baktaman from the central Highlands, being painted in preparation for an initiation ceremony, 1981.

mentarity of male and female generative powers and on the outward public presentation of masculinity rather than its private reinforcement. While it has long been recognized that rituals and particularly initiations involve moments of separation and reincorporation, in this case the art forms themselves – both the elaborated bilums and the body decorations – contain the hidden truth of the ritual: success, growth and fecundity can only follow from the combination of red and white (female and male) elements.

The feathers connote the larger process of growth that the initiate is understood to undergo. Among both cassowaries and hornbills, male birds actively feed the young in the same way that men act as ritual mothers, to complement or succeed women's role as natural mothers. The life cycle of the hornbill mirrors initiation particularly closely in the sense that growth in the seclusion of the nest is followed by a moment of brilliant revelation. Men's house, birds' nest, bilum and womb are thus linked analogically. No simple account of gender hierarchy can be extracted from this. On the one hand, female powers are accorded an original precedence; on the other, male practices and masculinity are clearly glorified to the exclusion of women, despite the containment of female elements within them – and this is not to broach the question of how men and women interact and value each other in daily life.

Other elaborated bilums are not directly connected with initiation cycles, but similarly register both male and female powers. The pig's tail bag, worn in dance, incorporates the tails of wild pigs caught by successful hunters and is transmitted from father to son or mother's brother to sister's son, and thus bears a whole history of hunting accomplishments, connecting men across generations. These bilums typify artifacts that have no obvious narrative content to outsiders, but are valued primarily for the stories that are materially evidenced by each trophy.

The highest stage of initiation is associated with the acquisition of a cassowary feather bilum, which is the finest article of male adornment. Cassowaries are not easily caught, but the hunter is magically empowered by a red seed bilum, a small neck amulet bag woven completely around a seed. The seed is identified with women's menstrual blood, which is believed to blind magically the cassowary and lead it into a snare. The cassowary is particularly important because it is seen to embody both male and female attributes, to be capable of autonomous, parthenogenetic reproduction and to manifest Afek's unique and original completeness. The androgynous character of this completeness, and an acknowledgment on the part of men of the need for female fertility, is expressed again in the female associations of the seed amulet bilum, which is paradoxically requisite to the paradigmatically male activity of hunting: arrows similarly incorporate looped decorations made by women. The acknowledgement of complementarity, however, does not express a broader condition of sexual equality, and indigenous inequalities have recently been made visible in ways that were not possible before colonization.

Male–female relationships in Highlands societies have been transformed over recent decades by cash-cropping, wage work and Christianity; new forms and uses of bilums reflect the changing situation. Nylon and innovative techniques producing blocks of colour have created a new range of bright patterns that enable women to challenge the traditional male notion that feather bags are more aesthetically brilliant than women's unelaborated bilums. Bilums have also figured significantly in religious changes in the Telefol area. Since the late 1970s, a revivalist indigenous Christian movement has rejected traditional cult activities, and particularly the models of gender

103 Christian revivalist women subverting traditional male–female distinctions by wearing men's elaborated bilums in the way men do, 1984.

relationships that initiation projected. On at least one occasion, during a ceremony marking International Women's Day, women affiliated with the movement wore the feather bags previously associated exclusively with men, and even parodied modes of cradling sacred bilums, marking their knowledge of male secrets and their rejection of the traditional ritual and sexual order. The very art forms   103 through which a cultural logic was constituted and revealed therefore now enable its subversion to be made explicit. It may be premature, however, to assume that the cult has been permanently abolished: as mining, Christianity and a path of modernization fail to deliver the wealth that was anticipated, a return to traditional practices, which has also been widely noted in the Sepik, is under way.

Some north Vanuatu mats would seem broadly comparable to bilums in their gender associations and transformations. Weaving is   104 done exclusively by women and is indeed an activity constitutive of womanhood, but the so-called 'money mats' of north Pentecost are beautifully dyed in magenta patterns by men, and become valuables exchanged by men. Early twentieth-century writers equated mats with money in a simplistic manner, but did note that their use was restricted to contexts such as the payment of bride price and the acquisition of rank in the 'graded society' referred to in the Introduction and elsewhere. Value evidently accrued to mats as they aged, and on Maevo they were kept in special huts and impregnated with smoke, producing a shiny black crust and eventually stalactites of ash and soot that were referred to as 'breasts', according to one traveller. This implies that despite the degree to which they appear to be 'overwritten' by male design and appropriated to a male realm, a feminine association is not only noted but directly equated with age and value.

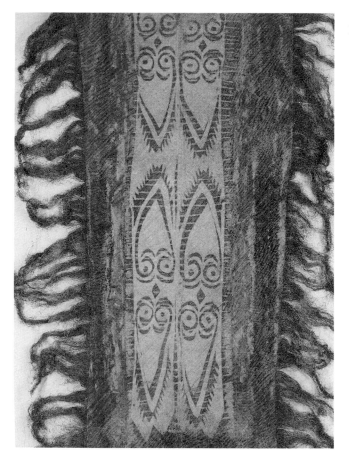

104 Detail of mat, Pentecost Island, Vanuatu, collected 1912. 12 ft 11½ in. × 33½ in.

There are other respects, however, in which north Vanuatu mats differ absolutely from bilums. While the latter are closely identified both with their makers and with a person for whom they are made, mats are incorporated into big ceremonial presentations; once received, the pile will be redistributed to re-enter exchange-paths at a subsequent event. While mats were and are highly differentiated on the basis of technical criteria, decoration, size and uses, they were not associated with their producers, nor were they individualized in the manner of some fine Tongan and Samoan mats, and *kula* shell valuables, the histories of which were known in detail. Their aesthetic efficacy emerged rather in the collective spectacle, in the prestigious appearance of abundance in a pile of mats assembled for a major presentation.

It is important to note, also, that the situation varied from island to island. Ambae mats were decorated by women rather than men, indeed the dyeing process was taboo to men, and women refrained from sex and observed various other prohibitions in preparation for it. The importance of dyeing was marked both by the fact that the log a woman used as a dyeing bath was said to become her canoe after death, when she would roam around the crater lakes of the Ambae volcano, the land of the dead, and by the fact that the same designs were dyed onto mats and tattooed onto women's legs; this suggests analogies with the parts of Polynesia in which tattooing shared both motifs and certain meanings with barkcloth.

It is notable that on Ambae there is a kind of women's counterpart to the male graded society. Women do not move up through a formalized hierarchy of named ranks, as men do, but they do draw together wealth, in mats rather than pigs, which are specially dyed and then presented to the woman's husband, who provides a return gift. These events are compared with male grade-taking by women and men, and women who have presented mats in this way a number of times are said to be 'chiefs among women'. Women's capacities to act as transactors in most north Vanuatu societies is limited and marginal; they are primarily producers, and are valued and respected, but not renowned in the way that men are. Renown is associated with rank, height and flight – traditionally male attributes that in Ambae women to some degree appear to share. The difference between Ambae and other parts of north Vanuatu is not merely marked by the fact that women dye mats in one place but not another: the capacity to produce and transact elaborated art forms itself *constitutes* what is distinctive in Ambae gender relations, politics and ritual.

Women's art forms have changed not only at the local level as a result of conversion to Christianity and other developments; they have a new significance in regional and national cultures. Although Telefol women among others have been unwilling to commercialize bilum production, bags are elsewhere produced for markets and for tourists.

105 (*above*) Distribution by bride's family of mats received in marriage exchange, Saraisese, East Ambae, 1992.

106 (*left*) The image of Papua New Guinea as Paradise is embodied in a bilum and offered for sale to visitors.

Looping techniques have spread into areas in which they were not previously known, and the bilum has become generically an emblem of Papua New Guinean identity and womanhood, and in its specific variants, a marker of regional identities within the country. In Vanuatu, as Janet Keller has shown, plaitwork and baskets in particular have similarly come to express both local and national identities. There, women's art forms are broadly akin from place to place and bear a range of locally specific and more general cultural connotations; these could be contrasted with male products, such as anthropomorphic images that refer more specifically to individual ancestors and cult figures. Men's art, like institutions such as the graded society, is therefore less readily translated or identified with beyond the immediate localities in which it is produced, while women's products more easily mediate perceptions of wider ethnic affinity. In markets and urban contexts, people acquire a sense of collective identity on the basis of a shared pidgin language, the use of artifacts such as bilums in Papua New Guinea and baskets in Vanuatu, as well as through shared food preferences, religious affiliations and practices, such as betel-chewing and kava-drinking. Given the cultural and linguistic diversity within the independent Melanesian nations and the political conflict that follows inevitably from extractive developments, such as logging and mining, and the growth of urban elites, it is likely that national consciousness within Papua New Guinea, the Solomons and Vanuatu will continue to emerge through shared practices and art forms in daily use, rather than at a more explicitly political level.

106
107

107 Basket, West Futuna, Vanuatu. Base 8¼ × 6¼ in.

108 Antoine Claude François Villerey, *Barkcloth making, House of Kraimokou, First Minister to the King, Sandwich Island, c.* 1819. 9¼ × 12⅜ in.

109 Tapa anvil, Marquesas Islands, nineteenth century. 6¼ × 6½ × 30 in.

CHAPTER SIX

Barkcloth, Exchange and Sanctity

If you were to have walked through almost any inhabited part of Polynesia in the early nineteenth century, or through certain valleys and villages today, the pervading sound might be not have been the wind through the breadfruit trees, or the surf against the reef, but the beating of barkcloth. The sound of mallet against anvil is a clear and resonant ringing that carries over considerable distances. According to one of the *Bounty* mutineers, Tahitian women, who usually made cloth in groups, sustained their beat to 'a Song given by one and Chorous'd by the rest'; they kept 'regular time . . . Shifting the piece backwards and forwards till it is all beat out to a regular Breadth and thickness' (*The Journal of James Morrison*). The musical tone was enhanced by the fact that the anvil, generally two to three metres long, was invariably of very dense and resilient wood. In eastern Polynesia it was not a solid block of wood but a low, hollowed-out trestle, a sounding-board supported on squat legs and in rare cases carved along the sides. Because cloth did not last long, and garments were of course always needed, cloth-making was continuously, aurally present in indigenous lives – not merely as noise, but as an expressive activity, and even a form of communication. In some places a percussion code was used to transmit messages, and in Hawaii the legendary character Kamoeau was said to be able to learn everything about a woman merely from having heard her beating. Even if most people would not have claimed to know a person's attributes from the sound of her anvil, this suggests that the process, as well as the final product, was of aesthetic interest, registering something of the producer.

Barkcloth is now known generically as tapa; the word is similar to the Hawaiian term *kapa* and to some terms for unprinted cloth or undecorated areas of barkcloth. As a generic term, it seems to have been spread with the lingua franca of travel and trade in the early nineteenth century, which is significant, because tapa designs changed a great deal over the period of contact with Europeans. The range of material in museum collections reflects not only localized traditions, in some cases flourishing up to the present, but also a history of cross-cultural stimulation, expressed most obviously in the use of tapa to produce garments of European, and especially missionary-favoured, patterns.

The cloth is made mainly from paper mulberry bark (sometimes from breadfruit and other trees) in most of Polynesia and in parts of western Oceania, notably in southern Vanuatu, the Solomons, coastal Papua and north-west New Guinea. While artifacts produced by women were often neglected by early collectors, and subsequently by the tribal art market, partly because they were classified as 'craft' rather than 'art', tapa has long aroused the interest of Europeans. Participants in the Cook voyages took it to mark the refinement of female work characteristic of the 'polished' societies of Polynesia, in contrast with women's seemingly more onerous agricultural labour in the western Pacific; in the nineteenth century, missionaries could represent tapa-making as a wholesome domestic craft untainted by the heathen imagery that was so conspicuous in other forms of indigenous art, though the most astute of them certainly understood that cloth did in fact possess religious significance, if only because refined forms of it patently marked the sanctity of chiefly men and women.

From the viewpoint of collectors, barkcloth differed from other art forms in the sense that it could readily be cut into small pieces, and from the late eighteenth century onward, albums incorporating sets of actual specimens, and in some cases a printed text describing the process of production, were compiled and circulated. While it remains valuable to know that these particular pieces were collected at an early date, such books exemplify the unfortunate tendency of ethnological collecting to split material and abstract it from its uses. A small piece of tapa ceases to be part of a garment, wrapping or gift of a particular kind, and can only be appreciated as a specimen of craft and ornament. The collecting exemplified in such compilations was, of course, especially concerned with decoration, mostly in unusual or distinctive specimens; this led to the neglect of undecorated cloth, which by no means indicated lower status in indigenous terms and which was extensively produced in some areas. More complex problems arise if the material is presumed to be purely decorative rather than conveying meaning, and this may be inevitable if all that can be seen are pieces or parts of pieces out of context, because the significance of tapa arguably arises not from 'meanings' that motifs may or may not possess, but from contexts of circulation and use.

The process of production would always involve various phases of soaking, scraping and beating the bark; in some areas a few days'

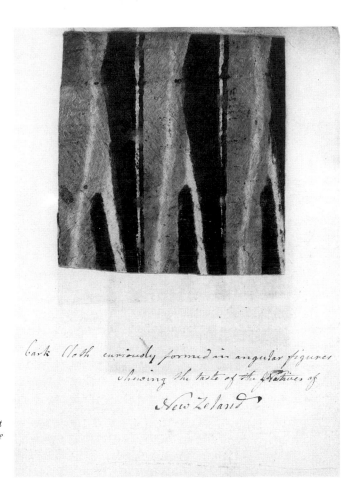

Bark Cloth curiously formed in angular figures shewing the taste of the Natives of New Zeland

110 Page from Alexander Shaw, *Catalogue of the different specimens of cloth collected in the three voyages of Captain Cook to the southern hemisphere,* 1787.

fermentation at an early stage was allowed to make the material more sticky and easier to beat into a cohesive sheet; supple and strong varieties were produced by beating out very fine sheets that were then pounded together; old tapa could similarly be repaired or joined to new pieces, but since the cloth was adversely affected by exposure, it seems more usually to have been simply discarded. The beater itself was square in cross-section and usually grooved, but in Hawaii and a few other places it was likely to have been carved with more complex patterns, leaving impressions in the cloth that might perhaps lie behind other designs, like watermarks in paper. There are many descriptions of the process; the missionary, Robertson, writing on the basis of late nineteenth-century observations, gave the following account of tapa-making in Erramanga, in southern Vanuatu:

The bark is taken off in broad strips, and done up in bundles. Then, on a round, smooth log, about a foot in diameter and eight or ten feet in length, one of these strips is laid. Generally two women work together at it, one on each side of the log. The 'beater' (*néko*) is made of *nokesam*, a very hard wood, which takes a high polish. With the exception of the handle, which is plain, it is often beautifully carved in patterns of leaves. Each woman has on the ground beside her a small canoe-shaped dish of fresh water and a whisk, made of reeds. Every now and then the bark is sprayed with water, and, after it is beaten for a long time, another strip is added overlapping the edge of the first one. The bark is so glutinous that in the constant beating the pieces join very quickly. As the women work, they draw the fabric from side to side of the log: strip after strip is added ... The colour is now a dull white, and the material very like parchment in appearance. It is hung over a bamboo or some creepers tied between trees, and while still damp, patterns are drawn on it with charcoal. The usual designs are the crescent moon (which seems to be used as a sign of and in connection with their sacred stones and heathen festivals), birds, fishes, lizards, flying-foxes, and usually the never-failing palm leaf and other leaves.

Robertson mentioned that one piece he was shown featured 'weird illustrations' of men – presumably European – on horseback: 'The artist was evidently a lady who moved with the times.' Such jocular and ambivalent responses to overtly non-traditional design are widely attested to. More important here are the broad similarities between Erramangan and Polynesian tapa-making methods. These arise in part from parallel solutions to similar technical problems, but point also to broad cultural affinities that existed and still exist across the Pacific, but that are easily obscured by regional categories such as 'Melanesia' and 'Polynesia' and by the particular features of local stylistic traditions. While Erramangan cloth certainly differed from western Polynesian material in the size of pieces and style, the material was not only prepared in basically the same way everywhere, but also possessed across the region related, if distinct, associations with the life cycle, kinship, ceremonial exchange and ritual.

There was much greater variety in modes of decoration than in production. Cloth was stained by immersion in dyes or mud; it was painted, stencilled, stamped and rubbed, mainly with vegetable dyes but also with ochres and soot; it was also directly exposed to smoke, sometimes varnished with resin, and occasionally perfumed. Speaking very broadly, staining, stamping with small motifs and free-hand painting prevailed in eastern Polynesia, while in the Samoa–Tonga–Fiji

111 (*opposite*) Barkcloth, Erramanaga, southern Vanuatu, late nineteenth century. 76 × 31–4 in.

112 Tapa from, top to bottom: Futuna, Tonga, Lau in Fiji and Hawaii.

area, more complex decorative techniques based on hand-painting and rubbing – and in Fiji, stencilling – were employed. In general, as would be expected, finer cloths, and the more finely decorated forms, were made specifically for those of chiefly status, or for ceremonial use.

Tapa was used in a range of garments, for marking tabooed places or property boundaries, for ritual purposes, such as the wrapping of a corpse, and on a large scale in exchange. Although the incorporation of barkcloth into elaborate sculpture is not widely attested to, painted human effigies were made from tapa around wood or wicker frames in the Marquesas, Rapanui and possibly parts of the Cook Islands; these were presumably for ritual purposes, which are not well documented. In Melanesia, the Baining people of New Britain also produce large and spectacular cloth-on-frame figures that are used in rituals, but this is again far less common than the use of tapa in clothing. While 'native cloth' was long abandoned in virtually all of eastern Polynesia (though now revived in Tahiti and Hawaii), its use

118

in ceremonial presentation, especially in the context of marriage, persists and indeed flourishes in Fiji and western Polynesia today.

In Tahiti, ordinary loin cloths and ponchos called *tiputa* were made 114 on a household basis, but in each district there was a very large house in which groups of up to several hundred women were occasionally recruited by those of high rank to produce large pieces of cloth for ceremonial presentations. A special form of undecorated tapa, known as *hobu*, was distinguished by its fineness and whiteness, which was produced by extensive bleaching in the sun. It was frequently compared to muslin by early observers and said to have been used for clothing by aristocratic women, but appears mainly to have been made in large sheets that were rolled into bales and stored in chiefs' houses. The wealth and status of an elite household was expressed in accumulations of cloth (as it was elsewhere in rolls of mats piled up above rafters); at death, the chief's body and the enclosure in which the body was displayed were wrapped in white cloth. Up to the time of contacts with 115 Cook and other mariners in the 1760s and 1770s, it would seem that other special forms of Tahitian cloth were dyed yellow or red but not actually painted; by the late 1790s, however, the influence of printed

113 Women of the Nalimolevu clan beside the clan meeting-house, Cakaulekaleka, in Ekubu Village, Vatulele Island, Fiji, July 1993. The occasion was a lifting of mourning ceremony three months after the death of a fellow clanswoman.

114 Chief of Borabora, Society Islands, wearing a tapa poncho, 1823. Note parallels between the barkcloth and tattooing motifs.

115 (*below*) John Webber, *Waheiadooa, Chief of Oheitepeha lying in state*, *c.* 1777–89. 16⅜ × 22¾ in.

fabrics prompted the Tahitians to expand the range of decorative techniques: pieces that were collected or depicted in the early nineteenth century bear printed fern leaf patterns and, significantly, motifs transposed from the range tattooed on the skin. Soon afterwards, calico and European garments were adopted on a wide scale and tapa abandoned. In a number of other places, such as Niue, the trend was similar, in the sense that a period of innovation and figurative representation was followed by a shift to imported cloth.

In Tonga, as in Tahiti, undecorated pieces of tapa served as everyday garments, and finer pieces of white cloth were used mainly by people of high status, especially for turbans. The pattern of production

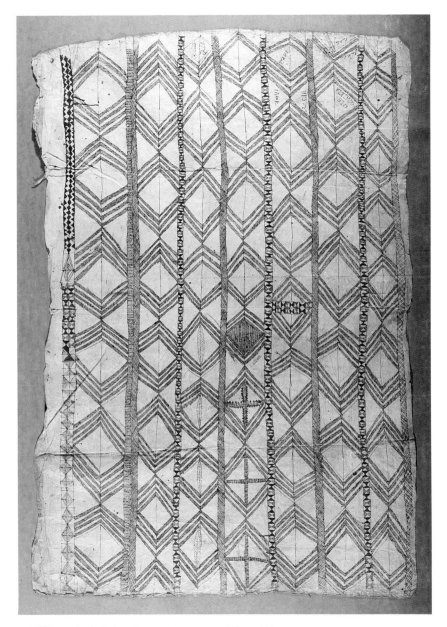

116 Niuean barkcloth, nineteenth century. 78¾ × 51⅛ in.

and use differed most strikingly from Tahiti in the sense that there was a much greater orientation towards production for exchange, and very large sheets were printed with the aid of tablets of leaf strips, bearing a whole range of triangular patterns and motifs based on leaves and flowers. The tablets were mounted on wooden half-cylinders and the cloth was rubbed, painted and pasted by groups of women, usually supervised and sponsored by women of high rank, in a production-line fashion that enabled the considerable demand arising from impending marriages, funerals and other ceremonies to be met.

While tapa-making in Tonga still proceeds in many respects along traditional lines, both the organization of work and the array of motifs have changed. Although the aristocracy retains much prestige and authority, introduced institutions have created new contexts for collective activity and elite women no longer control large-scale tapa production. Based particularly around the church, autonomous associations of non-elite women have gradually developed, and now most villages have one or several clubs, each with its tapa-making house. The leaf-tablet technique has been sustained, but the range of motifs proliferated to incorporate bicycles, ships, clocks, early gramophone record players and shooting stars. The fact that new motifs are regarded as the property of the originating women's club must have favoured innovation, but the elaboration of distinctiveness on the part of particular women's associations has not compromised deeper continuities or the recognizably Tongan character of the cloth. It is possible that the demand for tapa among Tongans in New Zealand, the United States and Australia has imposed a degree of conservatism, since those in the diaspora are likely to prefer material that stands unambiguously for their traditions and their ethnicity. In cities such as Auckland and Sydney, barkcloth can be seen in Polynesian markets, houses and churches, and it is intriguing that some of the most common motifs are crowns and lions, emblems of the Tongan and British royal families. The monarchist iconography seems to belie or mask the polite but insistent resistance to the aristocracy that may be as 'traditional' in Tongan society as the chiefly lineages themselves. This resistance is attested to over the past century, ironically, by the commoner women's clubs that now produce the barkcloth, and by the process of migration away from the island home that remains uneasily dominated by the royal family.

If, over recent decades, some imagery has become charged with political ambiguities of this kind, the meanings of the cloth arise, most importantly, from the way the material is used. Not all cloth was made

117 Theodore Kleinschmidt's drawing of Tui Nadrau, the chief of Nadrau (central Viti Levu, Fiji), wrapped in barkcloth for ceremonial presentation, October 1877.

to be given away, but very large pieces – sometimes of two or three metres in width and up to several hundred in length – were and are presented in the context of a variety of relationships, especially in western Polynesia, where the ceremonial exchange of valuables was in general more important than in eastern Polynesia (the emphasis there being rather upon the presentation of food and feasting). The idea that cloth is simply decorative misses the point that meanings arise from these relationships and transactions, rather than from symbolic content that designs incorporating abstract forms, plants, clocks or comets may or may not possess.

The ethnologist and collector, Anatole von Hügel, witnessed a presentation in the interior of Viti Levu, the largest island of the group, in 1875. These places were remote from the centres of Fijian power and wealth, and this would not have been an extraordinary presentation by Fijian standards, but the quantity of cloth offered was nevertheless considerable:

117

The Nabuto men had brought *masi* [cloth] as their gift ... The large *masi* bundles having been undone, the many hundred yards of stuff were first rolled into an oval ball, and then unwound from the ball and wound again on to the body of one of their own men, so that he had a huge encasement of *malo* [cloth] round him ... There was white *masi*, and some which on one side was silver grey, and also a thicker and wider sort, shiny and very dark, and mottled with black. This last variety was put on to another man in a succession of loops which fell in rows from his chin to the ground, and was so disposed at the back of his head to appear like a monk's cowl. When complete this strange garment made the wearer appear of enormous bulk, and the most extraordinary thing was that a single knot held the whole get-up together, which when undone allowed it to slip off in a mass to the ground ... Altogether there were five of these cloth bearers.

Von Hügel described the ceremony, which involved 'a solemn procession', speeches of offering and thanks, the presentation of whale teeth and subsequently the drinking of kava, but understood neither the relationship between the groups nor the particular purpose of the gift. It is probable, however, that the two parties were closely related through intermarriage, and that the recipients of the presentation that Von Hügel witnessed had at some earlier stage performed some singular service for the Nabuto people; they may have supported them in war, allowed them the use of some of their land, or even merely assisted one of their number who was ill in the course of travel. Any special help of this kind was understood to incur a debt that had to be repaid in manufactured valuables, such as cloth, mats and pottery, rather than through reciprocation by some similar favour. Although Fijians sometimes allowed debts to stand for years, they were understood to cause malaise if neglected indefinitely, and if a diviner attributed some particular misfortune to a particular debt, a group would have to make a presentation that extinguished their obligation.

It is also possible that the presentation was connected with marriage (although Von Hügel would presumably have realized this, had the occasion actually been the main presentation at the time of a wedding). The clan into which a woman married incurred a permanent debt to her natal group, marked by a succession of presentations, both at various stages of betrothal and marriage, and subsequently on the birth of her children. The child was not (and is still not) understood to be a self-subsistent member of a patrilineal group, but rather a kind of composite being, constituted by the nurture and substance of the mother's side as much as by that of the father. Presentations that mark these enduring asymmetries might be similar to those described by Von Hügel or they might involve a larger range of goods. Tapa was

142

presented not only in bundles that were wrapped around individuals, but also sometimes in long strips that were carried by dozens of individuals in line; and in some cases, long and wide strips were laid along the ground, especially for those of high rank to walk along.

These uses of the material are significant because, in many parts of the Pacific, the metaphor of the path is fundamental to the imagining of relations of alliance and affinity. The long strip of cloth gives material form to the path, but does more than make a relationship visible: its presentation by a long line of people also makes their collective action, and their very collectivity, manifest. Neither society in general nor a particular group such as a clan simply exist; a sense of collectivity cannot be present in people's minds unless a group somehow appears and acts as a whole. Its appearance and efficacy have to be stage-managed, and when people succeed in drawing their efforts together and making them visible on an occasion such as a ceremonial presentation, they may create something remarkable that they scarcely believe in themselves. It is in this context that collective products, such as large pieces of barkcloth, are especially important. The art form is part of a process of self-revelation and has a particular importance at a moment of presentation, when everyone's efforts converge; at other times, the cloth's significance may lie in the prospect or memory of such ceremonial events, or in a particular history of exchange-paths. The motifs printed on the cloth may refer to totemic plants, and may indeed be 'meaningful', but what is important about the art form, in this case, is not such 'meanings', but a presence that people can recognize as the result of their own action.

Tapa may be seen not only as a marker of debts of substance and nurture, but as a bearer of sanctity – and this may amount to the same thing, because, as Fijian women say, piles of valuables, such as cloth and whales' teeth, must be presented at marriages 'because a woman is a sacred thing'. When shamans wrap themselves in cloth to induce possession, or hang a long piece of cloth down the foundational post of their spirit house, the tapa evidently provides a vehicle for the deity's access or presence, and this is perhaps how the Rapanui and Marquesan cloth-covered figurines should be interpreted. The function of cloth to contain sanctity recalls the effect of tattooing to seal over the body and render *tapu* less contagious. It is not surprising that there should be an affinity, since, as Alfred Gell has pointed out, both cloth and tattoos constitute additional skins that are wrapped around individuals, and in some origin myths these skins are directly equated with the bark of trees used to make cloth. The significance of these

113

kinds of wrapping are, however, different, because cloth is often donned in order to be removed (as in the ceremonial presentation described by Von Hügel) and is therefore directed at the transmission of sanctity, or its temporary marking, rather than its insulation.

While the practice of wrapping the corpses of distinguished individuals such as chiefs in tapa is consistent with the accentuation of their sanctity prior to their departure for the land of the dead, barkcloth can also be used to dispel or disperse *tapu*; as was noted in the previous chapter, the intensely and threateningly sacred character of newly born children of chiefly status required that their *tapu* be diminished in a controlled fashion at successive times over childhood and adolescence. In the Marquesas this is apparent at the moment of birth, when a high-ranking woman would deliver her first child over the prostrate bodies of male kin, who lie beneath barkcloth sheets. When a chiefly girl first menstruated, she was secluded and subsequently reintroduced to the collectivity at a major ceremony. She was brought to this feast on the shoulders of close male kin and wrapped in tapa that extended around their bodies also. This way of presenting and honouring the woman was repeated at the time of her marriage, and perhaps on other occasions. In both these instances and that of giving birth, the fact that she is placed 'above' her kin suggests that her *tapu* is being reduced to the level of theirs, and rendering her less contagious, through the medium of the cloth. The significance of tapa in rituals marking the transformations of life can also be attested to by the ritual defloration of sacred Samoan virgin brides: the stains upon the barkcloth over which this was publicly performed were taken to demonstrate the bride's purity. In all the cases, the important point is not that the cloth or whatever motifs it bears represent gods, *tapu* or any particular form of relatedness; it is instead that the material helps bring about transformations between divine and human realms, marks advancement from one phase of life to another, and desanctifies peoples and objects when this is desired.

119 The barkcloth from the small western Polynesian island of Futuna, north-east of Fiji, is unusual for its surprising but unmistakable emulation of the design and appearance of woven mats from the Marshall
120 Islands. Though the latter are nearly 3000 kilometres to the north, the Marshallese had effective seagoing canoes, and it is likely that contact was made via the intermediate atolls of Kiribati and Tuvalu (formerly the Gilbert and Ellice Islands), before European contact. This reminds us that cross-cultural stimulation is not necessarily a matter of European influence, but has proceeded just as significantly through

144

118 (*opposite*) Tapa figure, Rapanui. Ht 16¼ in.

contact between indigenous cultures, in some cases over considerable distances. The mimicry of Marshallese patterns may contain some statement about political relationships or ethnic differences; alternatively, the women of Futuna may merely have found the designs exotic and distinctive. It is impossible to know.

Although barkcloth gave way to new, imported cloth almost everywhere in eastern Polynesia by the late nineteenth century, production was sustained into the early twentieth century on the island of Fatuiva in the southern Marquesas, which was preserved by relative isolation from some of the more destructive effects of French colonization. It was noted in the 1920s that tapa was still made on this island alone, and certainly from the 1960s onward, cloth was being steadily produced for sale to tourists, who tend to call at the island on yachting trips across the Pacific, reproducing the early patterns of exchange in giving tobacco and alcohol, and sometimes cash, in exchange for local artifacts and fresh fruit. The intriguing feature of contemporary production is the fact that cloth is not stained or decorated in a 'traditional' fashion – in fact, Marquesan cloth was occasionally dyed but never decorated – but painted with tattooing designs drawn from an

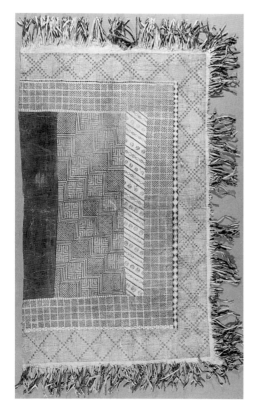

119 (*left*) Barkcloth skirt, Futuna, late nineteenth or early twentieth century. 62¼ × 38⅝ in.

120 (*above*) Costume mat, Marshall Islands. Late nineteenth to early twentieth century. 35⅞ × 35 in.

121 Barkcloth with patterns based on tattooing designs, Fatuiva, southern Marquesas Islands, *c.* 1984. 41⅜ × 35⅝ in.

ethnological publication, Karl von den Steinen's *Die Marquesaner und ihrer Kunst*. This appeared in the 1920s, and a few copies and photocopies of it circulate among tapa-makers in the valleys of Hanavave and Omoa. This activity, which might be disparaged as indigenous dependence upon an outsider's representation, is in fact arguably animated by the underlying affinities between cloth and tattooing. Among more popular images are full human figures that were reproduced by Von den Steinen from early nineteenth-century Russian accounts, but the motifs themselves have been more effectively reworked into powerful and elaborate symmetrical patterns. Though now produced largely for an external market, tapa of this kind is unmistakably Marquesan, and its local signature is likely to become increasingly important as identities and ethnicities in French Polynesia are affirmed in the wake of a long period of colonization that sought to impose cultural unity.

Where cloth was abandoned completely, it is not always appropriate to assume that a channel for indigenous creativity had simply vanished, and the richness of the culture diminished automatically.

On the contrary, in much of eastern Polynesia, and especially in the Cook Islands, the Society Islands and Hawaii, women's efforts were transposed to the making of appliqué and patchwork quilts, known as *tivaevae* or *tifaifai* (in the Cooks and Societies respectively). The initial stimulus was provided by missionary wives, probably New England women who worked in Hawaii from the 1820s onwards, and who almost everywhere encouraged indigenous women to take up needlework. Quilts are referred to by travel writers from the 1850s onward, and are conspicuous in late nineteenth-century photographs. Though functionally identified as 'bedspreads', they seem to be used frequently as backdrops behind people of high status, and are obviously items of display at ceremonies of various kinds. Floral motifs are by far the most common, and seem to have been prominent from an early stage, but geometric piecework is extensively produced in the Austral Islands, as are figures of Christ and pieces bearing the names of individuals to whom they were given. In Hawaii, flags and icons of the royal family convey pride in the distinctiveness of the Hawaiian heritage, a politically understated practice, but nevertheless an expression of widely held desires for some form of indigenous sovereignty within the United States.

123 Maria Teokolai and others, *Ina and the Shark, c.* 1990. 8 ft 5 in. × 8 ft 1⅛ in.

122 (*opposite*) *Ke kumum waina* (grapevine), appliqué quilt, Hawaii, before 1918. 7 ft × 7 ft.

Although early Hawaiian quilts often resemble those produced by white American women, some barkcloth motifs such as the star (reinterpreted in Christian terms as the star over Bethlehem) were transposed to *tivaevae*, as were the leaf motifs that had been copied from imported fabric onto Tahitian tapa by the end of the eighteenth century. As if to complete the circle, some pieces of late nineteenth-century Hawaiian barkcloth clearly imitate quilts by reproducing, in paint, the quadrilateral symmetry that arises from the process of cutting out motifs on a sheet of cloth folded into four or eight.

For the most part, however, appliqué quilts are entirely different to traditional barkcloth, mats and textiles in their methods of production and appearance. However, continuities emerge from their uses. *Tivaevae* are hung up like curtains and adorn houses, churches and spaces in which ceremonies are taking place. They are given to people of high status by being dropped before them or draped around them, in conformity with traditional presentations of tapa. In Niue and the Cook Islands, hair-cutting ceremonies mark a child's coming of age and are occasions for huge communal efforts, feasts and gifts of cash. Quilts beneath and around the child recall the use of barkcloth in the traditional desanctifications of children and adolescents at successive points from the time of birth up to around puberty. It is unlikely, however, that many contemporary eastern Polynesians would acknowledge sustaining non-Christian notions of *tapu*, and an open question remains as to whether its operation in this kind of ritual would still be widely understood. The practice of hanging quilts from church ceilings nevertheless suggests persisting associations with sanctity and rank, even if the old idea of contagious sacredness has been largely displaced by a generalized Christian holiness. Neither continuity nor cultural transformation should be exaggerated; on the one hand, the Polynesian world view has changed, but on the other, the connections between kinship, affinity, rank and elaborate forms of cloth persist. This is why any understanding of *tivaevae*, or tapa before it, as an essentially decorative, domestic or 'feminine' art form is fundamentally mistaken.

123

CHAPTER SEVEN

Feathers, Divinity and Chiefly Power

Hierarchical social relationships, based on criteria such as sex, age, and ritual seniority, have existed in all Pacific societies. In some areas, however, distinctions of rank were more accentuated, and the manifestly elevated status of chiefly families led Europeans to use the language of kings, queens and royal families. In so doing, they took particular artifacts to function as regalia, which was a legitimate identification in so far as classes of objects, or fine forms of ordinary things, were indeed closely associated with chiefly titles and people.

Anyone who rummages through museum stores is likely to be dismayed by the sheer number of items described as a chief's cup, staff, bowl or club, and in many cases these identifications were probably added by dealers or collectors long after pieces were collected in order to add something to their curiosity and market value. Among the range of art forms that really were connected with chiefly status and power in western Oceania are the fine greenstone axes of New Caledonia, displayed by chiefs in ceremonial processions before major feasts, and said to mark their authority and the fecundity and spirit of the tribe. These were, however, also used by people who were not chiefs, such as the rain-making priest, who would strike the soil

124 Carved stool, Cook Islands, nineteenth century. 5 × 16⅛ × 8⅜ in.

125 (*left*) Fly whisk, Samoa. Ht 20 in.

126 (*opposite*) Fly whisk, Tubuai, Austral
Islands. Ht 35 in.

ritually in the course of invocations. Artifacts of rank were more
elaborate in Micronesia and the eastern Pacific, particularly in the
markedly stratified societies of the Hawaiian and Society Islands, but
were produced to some degree everywhere in Polynesia. These
124,126   included beautifully shaped seats in the Cook Islands, fly-whisks in the
Austral Islands and the Societies, and feather capes and girdles, in the
130   Hawaiian and Society Islands respectively. Some of these forms were
associated only broadly with status, but others alluded directly to high
chiefly titles: to wear the girdle was to possess the title.

The European perception of regalia is misleading for these Pacific
cases in one crucial respect. Even if crowns and thrones are

iconographically complex, 'crown jewels' are on the whole only extremely valuable collections of precious stones and ornaments. Diamonds do not have properties or connotations that are peculiarly royal, and can be owned by people who have nothing to do with a royal family. An object such as a crown or mace is only a special ceremonial form of an element of armour or weapon that essentially could be marked in other ways. In Polynesia, however, feathers generally conveyed sacredness and were intimately connected with gods. Any feather artifact enhanced the efficacy and divinity of its wearer, and in the Society Islands, long feather sashes or girdles (called *maro*, like ordinary loin cloths) had associations with particular gods and former bearers and title-holders. The object, in other words, was not merely a sign but a material genealogy that connected divine ancestors and previous rulers with a living individual, as well as a substance charged with divine presence in itself. Sadly, no Society Islands girdle appears to have survived; many were probably destroyed around the time of conversion to Christianity, and one which was sent to the London Missionary Society vanished at some time before the Society's holdings were transferred to the British Museum in the late nineteenth century. A few Hawaiian feather sashes survive, but their uses and associations are unclear: the documentation, which is abundant in Tahiti, in the absence of the artifacts themselves, is in Hawaii curiously scant, though there is no doubt that girdles were closely associated with high chiefly titles and very likely to have figured in installation rites. The material and ritual parallels may stem from visits or migrations from Tahiti to Hawaii that took place, according to traditions and limited archaeological evidence, around the fourteenth century; these seem to have produced, or at least coincided with, transformations of the Hawaiian polity, toward a consolidation of chiefly power.

Sashes also figured in chiefly regalia in the Cook Islands and elsewhere, but were made of plaited pandanus rather than flax and feathers. The close similarities in design between girdle and basket patterns in this case incidentally reinforce the point made earlier, concerning women's cloth and plaitwork art forms. The importance of material of this kind has been diminished because their objects have been regarded as mere utensils, containers or garments, and associated with a domestic sphere (one which, in much of the Pacific, cannot anyway be credibly distinguished from a broader social domain). The evidence for intimate connections with sovereignty and sacredness is in fact abundant, even though, in the eastern Pacific case, it does not point to a specifically androgynous conception of divine power, nor a sense that male and female elements of chiefly power were necessarily complementary. It is possible, but not clear, that featherwork was made by women, but that male and female generative powers were not juxtaposed in eastern Polynesia in anything like a New Guinean manner. The identification of regalia as either a male or female form of art would be misleading.

For the people of the Society Islands, feathers were associated directly with origins and divine fecundity. The first being, Ta'aroa, had long existed in an absolute void, but after an eternity broke out through his shell to differentiate the heavens and the earth, light and darkness and a succession of foundations for the rock and earth (this was, as it were, the Polynesian Big Bang). Ta'aroa created other gods and shook off the red and yellow feathers that had initially covered his body: these 'became trees, plantain clusters, and verdure upon the land', in the words of a Boraboran recounter of the creation chant in 1822 (in *Ancient Tahiti*). Although certain plants and crops were identified with other particular deities, plant life in general is thus a transmutation of Ta'aroa's feathers.

This is significant because the most important element of Polynesian chieftainship was not political leadership, but the maintenance of a kind of auspiciousness manifest especially in agricultural fertility and more broadly in successful fishing and good health. Chiefs had a direct genealogical link with the ancestral deities who ensured growth and life, and thus possessed this special capacity and responsibility, but they were also connected with Ta'aroa in a non-genealogical way, by virtue of bearing the feather girdles that incorporated feathers derived directly from images of the god and, in a less immediate sense, from the god's original covering. This artifact thus condensed the epochal time of history and cosmogony into the simultaneity of divine presence.

Feather *maro* were crucial for changing political relationships as well as for perceptions of chiefly sanctity in general, because the highest titles and spheres of sovereignty were obtained only when a chiefly man or woman could be wrapped in the girdle or sash at the time of installation. The object itself consisted of a flax base which was progressively extended, as a section was added to mark each successive reign. Feathers, which were mostly red in the case of the highest *maro ura*, were sewn in individually with a human bone needle that remained permanently part of the girdle. Human sacrifices were made at various stages in the elaboration of the girdle and when the chief actually donned it and other insignia of the title.

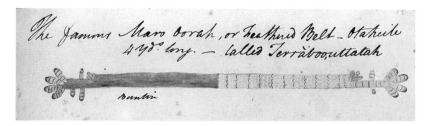

127 William Bligh, sketch of a Tahitian feather girdle, 1792.

On this same occasion, as was noted in Chapter 4, members of the Arioi society, whose decorations and sacrifices mimicked those of the high chief in certain ways, danced wildly and urinated and defecated on the king. Taken as an expression of sheer libidinous excess by the missionaries, this is intelligible in the context of notions of contagious sacredness discussed earlier: like the newly born, the newly invested king was profoundly and dangerously sacred, a condition that could be dispersed and diminished by actions of this kind which, like blood-letting and mixing, diffused the *tapu* state. The central feature of the ritual which produced this intensified sacredness was the wrapping in the girdle. After installation, the girdle was wrapped in barkcloth and a mat, and stored in a sacred house linked with the temple; it was only subsequently worn upon occasions such as the marriage of an heir-apparent, for meeting great guests and for sacrifices before war and at the conclusion of peace.

The feathers were apparently worked into checked patterns, although little more than stripes are visible in a sketch of one feather sash by William Bligh, Captain of the *Bounty*. It may have been the designs, or merely the division of the sash into sections associated with succeeding chiefs, that served a mnemonic function: in any case, the girdles were supposed to 'symbolize to the national chronicler the name, the character, and the acts of every monarch that reigned and the annals of the land which were faithfully recorded in chants and songs.' The main strip of the sash was divided at the end into a number of tongue-like extensions, which in one case at least are of the same number as the constituent tribes within the larger sovereign polity. It is not clear that this was always the case, and the lack of actual specimens and more precise historic information makes the suggestion speculative; but, given that the genealogy of the chiefdom is given

156

28 Feather gods, Hawaii, collected on Captain Cook's third voyage, 1778–9. Hts 24¾ and 40⅛ in.

material form, it may well be the case that its constitution through the union of districts was also made manifest.

Because possession of the girdle was identified with holding the title, and certain legends accounted for usurpation through seizure of feather *maro*, it is not surprising that the artifacts, together with other chiefly insignia and temple sites themselves, were considered peculiarly dangerous. Anyone touching or misappropriating feathers or even stones from the temple was supposed to be afflicted with ectropion, a disorder causing the eversion of the eyelids. This reversal of the proper relation between skins and organ is significant – given the politically charged Polynesian concerns with coverings, wrappings, skins, tattooing and cloth – but obscure. Insight, knowledge and vision were, however, as closely connected for Tahitians as they are in Western cultures, and the violation of sacredness generally resulted in blindness or some other visual disorder.

The particular political significance of the feather sashes emerges from complex shifts in political relationships and religious affiliations over the course of the eighteenth century, which were overlain and further complicated by European involvement in Tahitian affairs from the time of the visits of Wallis and Cook in the 1760s and 1770s. It is easy to attribute the rise of the Pomare chiefs in Tahiti to their close association, first with mariners, then traders and missionaries, and their ascendancy – like that of the Kamehameha line in Hawaii and the Bauan chiefs in Fiji – certainly was spurred on by the prestige and trade goods associated with contact. The fact that a new feather girdle was woven around a British pennant left on Tahiti by Wallis reflects the importance of foreign prestige, but also exemplifies the indigenous capacity to incorporate and manipulate the icons of colonial power that were just arriving on their beaches. The feather girdles thus suggest that to attribute the growth of the unstable nineteenth-century Polynesian kingdoms wholly to European influence would be to underestimate the significance of indigenous political dynamics.

Traditions suggest that in earlier phases of Tahitian political history, there was no link between chiefly titles and feather *maro*. When they were introduced is not clear, but those that were of the highest rank in the contact period were closely identified with the cult of the god 'Oro that spread from Raiatea in the leeward group of the Society Islands to Tahiti in the early to mid-eighteenth century. This took place as new *marae* dedicated to 'Oro were established on Tahiti and, most importantly, as a limited number of feather girdles were brought from Raiatea and Borabora.

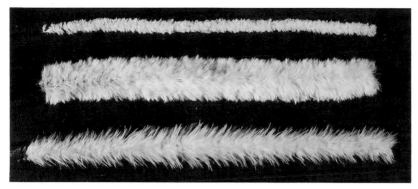

129 Feather *leis*. Ls 23, 24 and 25 in.

The particular association between the site of the Tahitian temple and the Pomare chiefs enabled them to claim the exclusive right to wear the *maro ura* – the scarlet girdle of the highest rank – while another chiefly family of Papara claimed the *maro tea*, the white or yellow girdle. It appears that the adoption of this form of insignia, together with a wider reorientation of local cults around the worship of 'Oro, created a differentiation of chiefly families and a consolidation of sovereignty that did not earlier exist. In other words, chiefly lines that had been relatively equal and autonomous came to be unequally ranked; perhaps at first primarily in terms of sacredness, but subsequently in terms of political and military power as well. The fabrication of the second *maro* may be seen as a sign of resistance on the part of the Papara chiefs to the emerging pre-eminence of the Pomares (though rivalries within and between chiefly lines at many levels did not always lead to the proliferation of insignia). Hence the idea that girdles were merely markers of rank dramatically understates their importance: they did not just reflect or express a wider political and social context, but embodied that context of political power in both generalized and specific ways.

Hawaiian featherwork was diversified, rich and beautiful. The intimate association with deities is manifest in feathered gods, notably powerful red effigies of the war god, Ku, and model temples, in which offerings were probably placed. Elaboration is, however, especially conspicuous in aristocratic garments and personal ornaments, collected in considerable numbers from the time of Cook's third voyage from 1776 to 1780, and now widely dispersed in ethnological

128

130 (*above*) Feather cape, Hawaii, collected on Captain Cook's third voyage, 1778–9. L. 50¾ in.

131 (*left*) The blackish-green feathers used in these *kahili* are from the frigate or man-o-war bird.

museums. Feather cloaks, shorter capes and helmets were worn by chiefly men of high rank, especially in warfare, and also by a few aristocratic women; feather *lei* were worn around the neck or as a hat band, mainly by women; and *kahili* were elaborated fly whisks, sometimes used as such and sometimes not much bigger than Samoan and Tahitian flaps, but also radically extended into a kind of vertical feather rainbow five metres or more in height. They marked the chiefly presence in houses, in processions and at ceremonies.

129
131
125

Despite their manifestly decorated appearance, capes and cloaks were in fact utilitarian items in the sense that they provided both physical and spiritual protection to their wearers during battle. Like the Tahitian girdles, the layers of feathers were understood to bear a chief's divinity and genealogies (recited as cloaks and capes were being produced); these presences no doubt awed opponents of lesser status. It might be suggested that feather wrapping enhanced a chief's divinity in a particularly powerful sense, given the widespread identification between cloth-covering and skin, the belief that founding gods' bodies had originally been covered with feathers, and the then current practice of making feathered gods. The line between gods and chiefs in Hawaii was indistinct in a variety of ritual contexts, and in war it is likely that a divinized chief, and one associated in particular to the war god, Ku, was all the more empowered. The godly character of the garments was enhanced by other elements, such as the use of sennit (coconut fibre or cord), which, all over Polynesia, was closely identified with deities and was in fact in Tahiti the material from which images of 'Oro among other gods were made. The idea of binding frequently had religious connotations as well, both negatively (in sorcery) and more positively, as when a divine presence might be tied into a canoe, a ceremonial adze, an effigy or a cape. There were thus many senses in which the making of these capes and similar artifacts installed and armoured sacredness; this, no less than the business of physically connecting feathers and fabric, was the essence of chiefly empowerment.

133

On a more practical level, cloaks and capes were made on a heavy base and densely covered in feathers, and would have provided some protection against stones and other missiles; the manner in which they hung loosely around the body should have done something to absorb blows. This cultural and material armature was of course not wholly efficacious, and the seizure of an enemy chief's cape in battle was a particular triumph that in some cases enabled the victor to proceed to appropriate the chief's domains and titles.

132 (*left*) Ku, God of War, Hawaii. Ht 78¾ in.

133 (*below*) Ritual adze, Mangaia, Cook Islands, collected 1891. Ht 12⅞ in.

134 (*opposite*) Decorated bottle gourd, Hawaii. Ht 8¼ in., Diam. 11 in.

As Adrienne Kaeppler has pointed out, the form of capes and cloaks appears to have changed over the late eighteenth and early nineteenth centuries. Firearms made the protective value of the cape obsolete and the garment evolved into an expression of genealogical rank. The colour red, which had been particularly associated with Ku and warfare, became less significant, and yellow feathers, which were rarer and more valuable and thus indicative more of wealth and status than sacredness, came into favour. Once the Hawaiians adopted Christianity, the manifold religious associations of capes began to diminish and they became more and more the emblems of rank that Europeans had from the start presumed them to be. Over the first half of the nineteenth century, fashions changed and chiefs adopted European garments, but *lei* and *kahili* continued to be elaborated, often using the feathers of introduced species, such as ducks, which were 135 more easily obtainable than those of rare parrots. While the political power of the royal families was constrained and appropriated by rapacious planters and settlers over the period up to American annexation at the end of the nineteenth century, the court continued to celebrate itself: among the fine artifacts that were innovatively elaborated are beautifully polished calabashes and decorated gourds and, as was the 134 case with barkcloth, floral motifs were added to the older range of geometric designs.

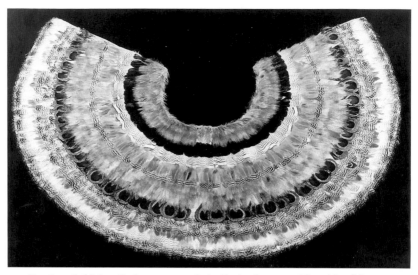

135 Duck and chicken feather cape, made in England *c.* 1824. The visit of the Hawaiian royal family to London in 1824 had a brief but popular impact on society fashion. W. 28 in., L. 22½ in.

From 1874 onwards, the erratic King Kalakaua attempted to revive a variety of Hawaiian traditions and encouraged the making of new capes from chicken and duck feathers. While some of the customary practices, such as *hula* dancing, remained vigorous and continue to be significant today, cape-making was only briefly re-established. This must be because the capes were, in the perceptions of many Hawaiians, too closely associated with the most exploitative and overbearing side of the traditional polity. The early capes embody a quantity of labour that is simply extraordinary, not merely in Pacific terms, but in any frame of comparison. Most were made from the very small tuft feathers of a few species of forest birds that produced a beautiful, even velvet texture. Some species were trapped by specialist hunters, selectively plucked and released; others had to be killed. Cleaning, binding and tying was a slow process; larger capes that consisted mostly of tiny yellow feathers might contain up to half a million, extracted from between eighty thousand and ninety thousand birds. Once again, the artifact underlines the nature of the polity. Nothing like these cloaks could have been produced in any other Oceanic society, because nowhere else did chiefs have the power to enforce such onerous demands upon their subjects.

CHAPTER EIGHT

Narrative Art and Tourism

It is often assumed that tribal art expresses the commemoration of ancestors and the representation of clan spirits. The canonical pieces are therefore masks or carvings that are supposed to stand for such figures, and the idea that Pacific art might incorporate narrative – as European history painting dramatized incidents of moral, political and mythical import – would seem improbable from this perspective. Ancestors and deities, however, are important not simply because they are dead or divine, but specifically because legends concerning their accomplishments frequently account for the ways in which life, work and political relations are organized; they might describe the origins of a society, in the case of creator-beings and founding ancestors, or in a localized sense, tell of more recent human ancestors, whose deeds are often the basis of claims to land, rank or ritual authority. This is not to say that myths work in a mechanistic way to 'explain' fundamental social relations, such as the gendered division of labour, or to justify the privileges of the elders or chiefs who might primarily be those who know and relate narratives. Although contrasts between male and female powers, the origins of rituals and the statuses of particular lineages are frequently at issue in myths and historical narratives, these stories often express moral ambiguities and, like the Christian scriptures, are potent because they can be drawn upon to support diverse and conflicting views.

Given that narratives of various genres are often prominent in both oratory and everyday talk in Oceanic societies, it would not be surprising if art forms that possessed no obvious narrative content for an uninformed outsider were, nevertheless, understood as bearers of stories. This can even be true of objects that do not represent the deities, protagonists or places that figure in myths and traditions: Queen Salote of Tonga said, 'Our history is written in our mats', referring to the exchange relations, kinship bonds and links between aristocratic titles that would be connoted, to the knowledgeable person, by particular fine mats. These artifacts bear their histories, as do Maori 136,138 *taonga* (treasures) and high-ranking Trobriand shell valuables.

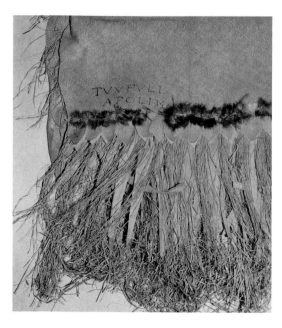

136 Detail of fine mat with feather
fringe, Samoa. 60 × 60 in.

Some Oceanic art forms do, however, denote rather than connote narratives, in greater or lesser detail. The constitutive or foundational character of an ancestor-deity's acts may occasionally be made visually explicit, as, for instance, is the case with 'A'a in the Austral Islands, whose role as generator of a plethora of other beings is marked in the smaller figures attached to the god's body; in Maori carvings, similarly, supplementary figures and artifacts condense references to genealogies and events. These examples are at the more allusive end of a continuum: in New Caledonia, Belau, the Solomon Islands and in isolated cases in Papua New Guinea, stories are represented in a more specific and detailed fashion, in images of war and seduction, encounters with divine and monstrous beings, meetings and transactions with colonizers and jokes at the expense of one's neighbours – although the relevant narratives are not always easily discernible in the absence of contextual information. The connection between the narration of the past, which was more widely practised orally, and visual art, was conspicuous particularly in facade and interior paintings in Palauan houses, which have been adapted over the last fifty years in portable forms for a tourist market. These art forms therefore raise not only questions about how histories are given visual form in the Pacific, they also raise the issue of the ramifications of commercialization.

Belau (formerly the Palau or Pelew Islands) is the western-most

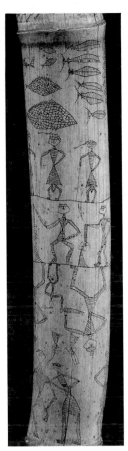

137 (right) Figure of deity, A'a, Rurutu, Austral Islands, collected 1820. Ht 44 in.

138 (far right) Detail of engraved bamboo tube, New Caledonia.

139 (below) Loom-woven textile, attributed to Kosrae, Caroline Islands, nineteenth century. 9 ft 1½ in. × 8⅝ in.

archipelago in the Caroline Islands, and like the rest of western Micronesia, appears to have been settled from insular south-east Asia directly rather than via Melanesia; the cultural influence of that area is manifest in forms such as loom-woven textiles (which were not produced on Belau, but highly elaborated in other parts of Micronesia, such as the Marshall Islands) that are otherwise absent from pre-European Oceania. All Micronesian societies were hierarchical, but rank in Belau particularly was organized in a complex, non-centralized way that confused Europeans. Chiefs monopolized various forms of imported glasseous and ceramic bead 'money', some of

139

which amounted to a kind of regalia in that they were permanently associated with particular aristocratic houses and titles. Others were alienable and were used as presentations at customary ceremonies to make alliances, reward warriors and compensate for offences; the manipulation of these valuables was really the substance of political life and remains important today.

Villages belonged to districts in which one village was pre-eminent, but both central and subordinate villages possessed, as they still possess, their own chiefly titles, men's and women's clubs, and councils. Elements of the polity thus were and are clearly centralized and hierarchical, but ranking coexisted with balanced or competitive oppositions between 'sides' of a village, 'sides' of an island, and so on. A model of complementarity between sides also extends to gender relations, male work being identified with the sea, while women are primarily concerned with taro gardens. A further dimension of social organization lay in relationships between four terms – four chiefly houses, titles, or villages – which in some cases were and are imagined as siblings and differentiated accordingly on the basis of birth-order and sex.

These principles did not cohere in one indigenous conception of society and political relationships, but were drawn upon in different contexts, and entered in varying ways into the collective houses

48,140–5 known as *bai*, in which the four cornerposts provided the key structural supports. Seating positions were precisely defined: certain titles corresponded to each cornerpost, and members of village 'sides' faced each other across the longer axis of the house. In larger villages, there were several kinds of *bai*, including two or three associated with chiefly councils, others belonging to clubs – often of non-chiefly warriors – and one or two more that might house visitors, or be appropriated to the use of visiting groups of women: these women were referred to as 'concubines' in European sources, and they exchanged sexual favours for valuables, usually because they aimed to accumulate traditional money that they would take back to their home village.

Only the chiefly *bai* were elaborately decorated, and, as might be expected, their ornamentation directly expressed the prestige and wealth of the chiefly group. The mediation of money was marked in the construction, since they were built not by a chiefly family or its dependents, but usually by renowned carpenters from allied villages, who were paid in valuables. Bead money is conspicuously represented

141 in motifs that border the narrative images on *bai* facades: the incorporation of one of the money symbols into a Janus-figure (on a

168

140 (*opposite*) Bai, Airai, Belau, Caroline Islands.

141 Detail of a money motif from a *bai*, Belau, Caroline Islands, collected 1909.

bai now in the Hamburg Museum) is particularly significant, given the wide association between two-headed figures and emblems of divine and chiefly power elsewhere in Oceania, which I have discussed in several earlier chapters. The capacity of such figures to see everything, the absence of a point of vulnerability, is in the Palauan case condensed with the prime medium of value and the means through which chiefly accomplishments were brought about.

These houses were almost certainly constructed before the first extensive European contacts with Belau in 1783, when Wilson and the crew of the *Antelope* were wrecked there. They established good relations with the high chief, Ibedul, constructed a new vessel, and left considerable numbers of iron tools on the island. It is likely that newly available iron tools led, as in New Zealand, to an elaboration of construction and decoration, but engravings depicting *bai* very similar to those still being constructed in the early twentieth century, were published as early as 1790. The 1790 account not only illustrated *bai*, but described them as 'the most astonishing fabrics that we ever beheld considering the tools and workmen that constructed them ... The beams are laid about seven feet high above the floor, curiously carved, and so nicely fitted to the supporters that appear as one piece of timber ... The inside of this house is most curiously worked and ornamented with various flowers and figures. The ends have much appearances of Gentoo [Hindu] temples' (*A Supplement to the Account of the Pelew Islands*).

The German ethnologists, Augustin and Elizabeth Kramer, were able to document over 150 *bai* from 1908 to 1910, but virtually all were destroyed over the next half-century as a result of typhoons, conflict among Palauans or in the course of the Second World War. In recent years, chiefly councils and clubs have come to use wooden and cement meeting-houses; some neo-traditional *bai* have been built, generally incorporating pan-Palauan histories rather than the localized perspective of a particular chiefly group. At least one of these, however, was destroyed during the political strife around Belau's nuclear-free constitution and relationship to the United States: the fact that *bai* might be arsonists' targets ironically attests to their continuing importance as expressions of Belauan political relationships.

The distinctive feature of *bai* art is painting in red, yellow, black and white ochres on low relief or rather a surface into which outlines have been cut. *Bai* always feature money, chicken, clam-shell icons and

142 Engraving after a 1790 sketch of a *bai*, Belau, Caroline Islands, 1803.

143 *Bai* facade, Belau, *c.* 1908–10.

144 (*left*) Figure of the goddess Dilukai from a *bai* facade, Belau, Caroline Islands, collected by Augustin Kramer, *c.* 1908–10. Ht 25⅞ in.

145 (*below*) *Bai* facade, Belau, *c.* 1908–10.

usually also a representation of the god of *bai* construction. The facades at both ends are decorated, as are both sides of crossbeams internally. In some cases the entire facade is taken up with one image, but more typically each plank, and sometimes the left and right halves of a plank, forms a separate panel that refers to a distinct narrative; a succession of linked images in a comic strip effect is also documented. This is consistent with the finding of an ethnographer in the 1970s – that there appeared to have been few strict rules about the formal organization of *bai* images and motifs. There seems to have been a similar degree of flexibility in the narratives represented, which ranged from foundational myths of origin to funny and insulting depictions of rival groups' misadventures. Others relate to recent incidents and European contacts are conspicuous in some of the *bai* facades photographed by Kramer. It is unlikely that Palauans made rigid distinctions between history and myth, although they do distinguish between a number of epochs: an early time marked by the creation of the islands and the political relations inaugurated by Chuab; a subsequent period in which the children of Milad founded the four capital villages of the modern Palauan polity and recent times marked by successive Spanish, Japanese and American colonial regimes.

146 A myth depicted on many *bai* concerns a breadfruit tree with magical properties. A woman, Dirabkau, who lived childless on an atoll, discovered an egg that swelled and eventually broke, as a child of the sun emerged. The youth grew up and was the first to hold a certain customary feast in honour of his wife, the daughter of a chief. The youth, named Terkelel, had long wondered why his adopted mother subsisted on a monotonous diet of breadfruit and asked her why she ate no fish. She replied that she was poor and there was no one to provide it for her; her neighbours walked past her house every day as they returned from fishing, but never offered her anything they had caught (or, in another version, they had abandoned her when they moved away to another village site). He was sorry for her and dived beneath the island, swimming up into a breadfruit tree that grew before her house; he cut a hole through the trunk and the thick branches so that the waves and rising tide always threw fish through the hole and out in front of her house. Others in the vicinity became jealous of the woman, who only had to sit under her tree to have an abundance of fish, sufficient even to distribute to her greedy neighbours. Why should the men have to venture forth in their canoes and the women slave away in the taro patches? Finally, their envy overcame them, and they cut the tree down, but once it was broken open, the

146 Storyboard depicting the magical breadfruit tree, Belau. 8¼ × 23¾ in.

water that had flowed intermittently burst through, and the whole island was flooded. Only Dirabkau herself was saved by Terkelel, who placed her on a raft and flew through the sky himself to join her again.

The social condition described at the initial stage of the story is plainly abnormal: the woman, who is without a husband and without children, is sustained by breadfruit rather than taro, the usual focus of women's gardening, and is not supported by her neighbours. In other words, the conventional balances between male and female, and the cyclical, mutual nurture of older and younger generations, are lacking, but are redressed in a radical way by the semi-divine son: equally out of the ordinary, the woman obtains both male and female food without labour. While her neighbours have previously neglected the responsibilities of kinship by failing to provide for her, the old woman now provides for them, but their selfishness and jealousy, however, bring about their destruction. Obvious morals are present: one should care for the aged, and – rather as in the European fable of 'the goose that laid the golden eggs' – greed is self-destructive. Such general injunctions and warnings are, however, probably less important than an affirmation of the necessity of complementary division of labour, through which male and female production, associated with sea and land respectively, contribute mutually to a kinship economy. Sociality is presented not as a natural order that people can take for granted, but a fragile condition to be defended against dispositions and behaviour that undermine it. From this perspective, the old woman's absolute self-subsistence threatens reciprocity as profoundly as does her neighbours' selfishness; it is an impossible condition that is perhaps necessarily put to an end by their action, which may be right or inevitable despite its overtly destructive character.

The story of the fish-bearing tree has both a particular and generalized significance that emerges from the subsequent fortunes of the female character. In some versions, the son Terkelel steals a stone figure belonging to the gods; in others, a god's eye is stolen and subsequently made into the money that is the crucial medium of Palauan exchange and political life. In either case, the gods are enraged and send seven messengers in search of the thief. They leave some fish with the woman, asking her to prepare it for them; she is in the process of cooking her own taro, and splits each piece, placing a fish between each half. The messengers later return, and on unwrapping the cooked parcels, are at first angry because they believe that the woman has taken the opportunity to eat their fish and has given them her taro in its place, which would be understandable because she has no husband and no fish; but they are delighted when they discover the concealed but particularly appetizing combination. As an expression of gratitude, they tell Dirabkau that the god will send a flood as punishment for the theft, from which she alone can escape by building a raft. Her son, however, makes the raft inadequately, and she floats away on a taro pounding-board, and is later drowned. The messenger spirits are distressed and seek ways of bringing her back to life; after several unsuccessful attempts, they induce a reluctant spirit to occupy her body between morning and evening; this explains why people need to sleep while the soul wanders at night. Now called Milad ('she who was dead'), the woman bears four (or in some versions, five) children, who found the major villages of Belau, namely Imeungs, Ngerkeai, Oreor and Melekeok (and sometimes Ngebei); their names refer variously to characteristics such as stubborn haughtiness and restless energy, which are appropriate to the rank of first and subsequent siblings.

The sequence of myths is clearly foundational in several senses: it accounts for the origin of basic human characteristics (the need to sleep), basic institutions (such as the use of valuables) and, perhaps most importantly, for political relationships between the four 'cornerposts' of the Palauan polity. It further recalls the structure of the breadfruit tree story in the sense that transgression leads to a flood; the ideal of male–female complementarity is expressed again in the distinctly palatable combination of fish and taro, for which Dirabkau is rewarded, ultimately, by being brought back to life.

The Milad stories convey much more than admonitions against selfish behaviour: they also image narratives about gender, sociality and siblingship, which define ideals and create terms for argument about actual relationships. At least two hundred other narratives figure in traditional *bai* paintings; some of these are less evidently of mythical significance than tales that mock the stupidity or gross behaviour of the people of rival villages and districts. Many incidents of contact with European and Japanese colonizers are also manifest in images of ships, cargo, cranes and people; like indigenous historical knowledge itself, the art constituted anything other than a closed system.

From the late nineteenth century onwards, a few *bai* paintings were cut from houses to be given to foreigners, and in the 1930s a Japanese scholar and artist encouraged Palauans to reproduce the carvings on smaller pieces of wood that could be sold to tourists. Japanese buyers often had some familiarity with traditional Palauan art and there was initially great emphasis upon the production of 'authentic' replicas, but after the war storyboards were sold primarily to Americans, who were less preoccupied with conformity to tradition; consequently more innovation took place. The combination of paint and incised lines still seems to be predominant, but boards have also been carved in relief without paint, and even in the round. This diversification of techniques may have been in response to visitors' expectations that indigenous art would take the form of carving rather than painting. A more naturalistic approach to the human figure is notable in the work of some carvers, though others appear to have been inspired in different directions by American comic strips. Exaggerated penises, particularly in the context of narratives concerning seduction, warfare and rape, are common and there seems to have been a fortuitous match between the predilections of military and tourist buyers and an erotic element in the traditional iconography, which was elaborated on demand.

In conformity with a very general rule that signs of contact and modernity are taboo in tourist art, the representations of cargo ships and white men with their bottles and pipes drop out of the corpus completely. There is a shift to images that can be taken to be emblematic of Palauan life; a number of boards, for example, figure not stories but the *bai* itself, with one or two coconut trees, and this image is significant not only in representations intended for sale to outsiders, but also in constructions of Palauan nationality for Palauan consumption, in official insignia, for instance. Stories popular on boards include some of deep indigenous significance that are accessible at least on a superficial level to outsiders, such as that of the fish-bearing breadfruit tree, and others marked primarily by visually dramatic, picturesque or erotic content. One popular narrative concerns the killing of a

147 Storyboard depicting the tale of the dissatisfied wife, Belau. 6¾ × 25 in.

monster that preyed upon villagers cooking fish; others tell of ingenious husbands who use trickery to discover their wives' lovers; and one concerns an unsatisfied woman who was sent by her husband to find a man with an exceptionally long penis, shown extending across the waters of a lagoon.

The storyboards raise wider questions concerning value and expression in art produced for tourists. A conservative, purist view assumes that the most authentic tribal art is that produced prior to contact with Europeans, that technological change (the introduction of iron tools, the use of imported paints rather than indigenous dyes and so on) leads to quicker, slipshod production, and that work produced for sale, particularly work produced on anything like a mass basis for sale to tourists, is of negligible cultural significance. The view that cultural decline or extinction followed from contact with the market tended to be sustained both by endorsers and critics of colonialism; the latter were often moralistic and had little doubt that they knew better than the confused or misguided 'natives'.

Cultural contact is no longer regarded so pessimistically. If much certainly has been lost, the resilience and vigour of indigenous and postcolonial cultures is simply too conspicuous for the 'fatal impact' view to be sustained. The interest and importance of neo-traditional work is consequently now more widely appreciated by curators and by the tribal art market, even if disproportionate value is still placed upon work that appears to predate contact. At the other extreme, it can be claimed that all forms of cultural production are equally valid and meaningful; and, given that much fine European art was produced for a market, there need not be an antipathy between commercialization and quality.

Storyboards suggest an intermediate position that neither dismisses nor endorses tourist art uncritically. On the negative side, what can be expressed has diminished, both in the sense that the range of narratives depicted has contracted from the hundreds to around thirty, and in the sense that their evocative complexity has been reduced. In part, this is simply a result of decontextualization. A whole corpus of stories is no longer integral to an occupied house, a structured place for formal gathering and political debate, a locus of village affairs and prestige, within which narratives are drawn upon for one implication or another. Stories instead become separate units that have a one-to-one relationship with a painting or carving; they stand not for their own internal complexities and ambiguities, but become emblems of Palauan folklore and are reduced to brief texts that are circulated in photo-copied form and sold with the artifacts. Even if particular stories sustain much of their original significance in the minds of the artists, they are produced in a folkoric form in order to appeal to tourists, and can only end up being conceived in that form by their producers. This would not necessarily be so if the art forms actually had indigenous uses before they were sold, as pieces such as Asmat *bisj* poles and New Ireland *malanggan* do. In both these cases, carvings produced for mortuary rituals, which were formerly disposed of after the ceremony, are now sold: a market is provided for without a radical reorientation of artistic

68
25

148 Breadfruit tree billboard, erected during the campaign for the first plebiscite on the Compact of Free Association between the United States and Belau, 1983, with American funds and programmes replacing the fish that would have magically burst forth from the tree in traditional versions.

149 Storyboard, attributed to Simon Novep, Kambot village, Keram river, Sepik Province. 39⅝ × 63 in.

production. In the Palauan case, however, the scale of work and the nature of indigenous use render sale and indigenous use incompatible.

Against this, it needs to be noted that some stories remain highly salient within Palauan political life. The magical breadfruit tree, in particular, has been reproduced on billboards in the course of debate about the 'compact of free association' with the United States, which dragged on through the 1980s and 1990s. The story is especially potent because it can be claimed by those on both sides of the debate: Belau's natural environment may be seen to be sacrificed for greed and money, from one perspective; from the other, a ready flow of financial benefits may be cut to pieces by the selfish actions of a few. Although the moneybags do not appear in tourist art, the traditional breadfruit tree remains resonant: it is not insulated from the more contentious imagery of contemporary politics. Despite commercialization, Palauan narrative art therefore retains expressive power, and even the capacity to tell and make history that was built into the *bai*.

So-called storyboards are also made in the Kambot area, on the southern side of the Sepik in Papua New Guinea. These distinctive openwork carvings have no obvious antecedents in the traditional art forms in the area, and curiously, the closest parallels are in filigree

148

149

150 (*right*) Detail of paddle, Buka, Papua New Guinea. Ht 67 in.

151 (*far right*) Detail of paddle, Buka, Papua New Guinea, c. 1900. 50 × 4½ in.

plaque ancestor figures, from Maprik villages such as Roma, further up the Sepik on the northern side of the river; travel associated with plantation work may possibly have brought Kambot artists into contact with Maprik carvers or their products. They have been produced specifically for sale to tourists since the 1960s and have proved popular, partly because they are portable and readily mounted on walls, but also surely because they convey something exotically simple that appeals to collectors. The most prominent figures are usually crocodiles and groups of men paddling canoes, and it is probable that myths of origin and migration are referred to, although the meanings attached locally to the carvings have not been documented. Schools of fish, lizards and snakes constitute a dense and active background, but it is interesting that some of the more elaborate examples depict villages stereotypically, with women, houses, pigs and coconut palms, suggesting that there has been a conscious effort to cater to the tourists' interest in scenes of indigenous life. Most boards at least loosely employ Western, perspective-structured representation, and it is likely that the carvers have drawn upon illustrations in school or mission books. Narrative may also be directly prompted by the circumstances of cultural change: this appears to be attested to by a remarkable dance paddle from Buka that bears an image entirely unlike the conventional, symmetrical anthropomorphic forms found on hundreds of examples from this part of the northern Solomons in museum displays and stores throughout the world. This poignant image of a child about to be sacrificed, from around the end of the nineteenth century, is likely to have been stimulated by a government or missionary campaign against the practice, which led to its ban.

151

A tie beam from Uki Island in the south-east Solomons, collected by Julius Brenchley in 1865, provides a further example of indigenous narrative art likely to have been produced in the absence of exposure to Western models. As in other parts of the Solomons, canoe houses were also men's cult houses, and contained valuables, heads and carvings presumed to represent ancestors or deities. Houses on Uki and San Cristobal also seem to have been painted internally and this beam bears on one side projecting relief carvings of bonito, sharks and frigate birds; as was noted in Chapter 3, bonito fishing was highly ritualized, and of such importance that male initiation was defined essentially as the induction of boys into the art of fishing; frigate birds were important both because they accompanied bonito schools and because their predatory characteristics were valued. It is the other side of the beam that has more of a narrative character: four canoes are engaged in

152

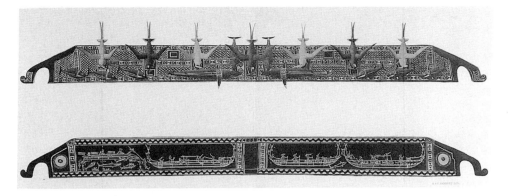

152 Tie-beam from custom or canoe house, Uki Island, eastern Solomon Islands, collected 1865. L. 15 ft ⅛ in.

fishing, one of which has capsized, with the result that its occupants are being eaten by sharks. Brenchley speculated that these unfortunate individuals had failed to propitiate the sharks with customary offerings; this may conceivably have been intended, although it is more likely that the beam depicts particular canoes and fishermen rather than merely a generalized cautionary tale. This is, however, precisely the kind of information that is no longer available.

These examples establish that Oceanic art was never limited to a single modality, as expectations about the functions of 'tribal art' within 'tribal religion' might lead one to expect. Art was certainly often intimately associated with cult activities, or with transmissions of sacredness, or with the statuses of powerful individuals; but the diversity of the 'religious' in itself, and its roots in political and sexual relationships and in historical transformations is easily underestimated. Some art forms were primarily connected with the propitiation of spirits; many certainly aimed to evoke their presences; but others were intended especially to narrate their deeds, as well as those of demigods, ancestors and even recent white intruders. Oceanic art possessed not a single, sacred mode, but found uses for genuine abstraction, figurative representation, the embodiment of ancestors and storytelling: it incorporated all these things and more.

CHAPTER NINE

National Independence, Indigenous Minorities and Migrants

New forms of art using 'Western' techniques and media have emerged in urban contexts in a number of Pacific countries. I have not called this 'contemporary art', because the baskets, body decorations and barkcloth that are still produced in many villages are no less contemporary; but the new art forms do emerge from particular situations of decolonization and address national and international audiences that traditional art never anticipated reaching.

The difference is not merely one of scale. Paintings and prints that are displayed at institutions such as the National Museum and Art Gallery in Port Moresby, and that tour Australia and Europe in travelling exhibitions, are indeed seen by larger numbers of people in more places than cult objects or paintings in village milieux. What is distinctive, however, is the way in which the art is taken to express the cultural vitality of a 'new nation'. A nation is not simply a larger version of a tribe; it is rather a peculiarly modern cultural entity that ideally possesses a distinctive character, which is somehow expressed both in the whole and by its constitutive individuals. However, the project of expressing unity or a collective 'spirit' may resemble the work of traditional aesthetics less superficially than might be anticipated. The form of sociality is certainly novel, but the project of making the nation visible is not so different to the evocation of collectivities of men, which was arguably at the centre of much of the art discussed earlier.

The first generation of independent politicians was fully aware that the project of making a Melanesian nation would be difficult, because most Papua New Guineans did then and would still see themselves, in most contexts, first as Chimbu or Tolai or Huli. They might also identify themselves in provincial terms, and even more generally, as Melanesians, while not necessarily carrying a strong sense of being Papua New Guinean. This is not a problem for people in many rural areas, and artists are not necessarily preoccupied with nation-making either. It is one, however, that national ideologues and policy-makers must address, and one of the ways in which they have done so is by

153 Martin Morububuna, *The Young Nation of Papua New Guinea*, c. 1978. 22 × 29½ in.

commissioning works of distinctively national art for new national institutions and state buildings. Even where artists' agendas have been more localized or personal, their works have often been assimilated to the project of representing Papua New Guinea for its elite, and in an international arena of cultural diplomacy.

Expatriates have frequently acted as catalysts for cultural revitalization and experimentation, and important early stimulus was provided in this case by Georgina and Ulli Beier, who had had experience in cultural affairs in Nigeria before coming to Papua New Guinea in the mid-1960s. They encouraged individual artists and pressed the new University of Papua New Guinea to set up a cultural centre that later evolved into the National Art School. By the time of independence in 1975, a number of artists had emerged, who were able to apply skills in sculpture and drawing to design and work on an architectural scale, which seemed to supply the distinctively Papua New Guinean signatures that new institutions needed. One of the most successful examples of design inspired by traditional styles was David Lasisi's concrete facade panels for the Papua New Guinea Banking Corporation, drawing on Papuan Gulf masks and shields. It is notable that the artist himself came not from this area but from New Ireland, and that today, sensitivities concerning indigenous copyright in artistic motifs and traditions might preclude an artist making so much use of the style of an area other than his own; the fact that there would at least be controversy itself marks a shift from the optimism that followed independence to a period of deep divisions.

The building most identified with the nation is the Parliament House, completed and opened in 1984. From the start this was intended to convey the distinctiveness of the country, without being dominated by art styles from any one region; consequently, a good deal of trouble was taken by architects and designers to incorporate references to all tribal groups in an expression of national unity. The building as a whole is shaped like a spearhead, and its most spectacular feature is the facade at its point, inspired in form by a Tambaran house from the Sepik, but more inclusive in its content. The range of the national environment is imaged in sea, earth, rivers and sun; men and women appear as partners, equal though differentiated by the spear and the bilum; traditional agriculture and fishing are depicted, but so is development; the cassowary and the helicopter capture the synthesis of tradition and modernity. A smaller, linked building is intended to suggest the circular men's houses of the Highlands, and as those are often used for feasting, this appropriately contains banquet and dining rooms. Internally, there are elaborate syncretic sculptures produced from the National Art School, which draw upon styles from many areas; the parliamentary chamber is dominated by a wall based on Papuan Gulf masks, while the high table in the state dining room has a panelled front by Martin Morububuna incorporating scenes of village life from across the country. A further office building has plaitwork-based geometric patterns that are supposed to symbolize the weaving together of the nation.

The building effectively draws both upon art forms resonant with esoteric, traditional powers, and those of everyday significance, such as the bilum; it could therefore be seen to represent heritage without alienating it from the people who are supposed to bear it and to whom it belongs. The many continuities in style and iconography between the House and neo-traditional rural art forms, such as the Kambot storyboards, suggest that the official imagery is not divorced from

163–4
155

156

154 Ruki Fame, *Man on Bicycle*, 1975. Ht 21⅜ in., W. 17¾ in.

widely shared perceptions of village life. In a more benign political environment, the Parliament House might really have become something with which citizens broadly identified; the problem has been that the 'diversity' that nation-builders recognized and attempted to endorse, has become a euphemism for widespread separatism and a failure of coherent government. The separatist war on Bougainville has only been the most obvious expression of the problem, and even if an independent state there is never internationally recognized, the decline of state control and legitimacy is such that Parliament House has come to express precisely what does not exist. The play of truth and illusion that always energized *haus* Tambaran is indeed reproduced here, but ironically: if there was always a risk of making the mystification of Arapesh sociality explicit, here collectivity has been revealed as a mystification before anyone had a chance to believe in it.

155 (*above*) Papua New Guinea Banking Corporation, Port Moresby. Designed by David Lasisi, 1976.

156 (*opposite*) Parliament House, Waigani, 1983.

157 Timothy Akis, untitled drawing, c. 1977. 40⅛ × 25¼ in.

158 Timothy Akis, *Palau na munuk* (cassowary and lizard), c. 1979. 29⅛ × 20½ in.

Although art has been drawn into the effort to produce a national culture, artists have always had more particular and personal concerns. Timothy Akis acted as an informant and interpreter for several anthropologists in the 1960s, and began sketching as a way of illustrating concepts he found it difficult to convey in pidgin. His work was encountered and encouraged by Georgina Beier, and subsequently developed rapidly; he produced many ink drawings before his death in 1984 that became well known in Australia and elsewhere through screenprints. Although he had experience as a plantation labourer and spent time in town, Akis's work was wholly devoted to traditional milieux and depicted creatures of ritual significance, such as cassowaries, flying foxes, snakes and lizards; anthropomorphic figures may be either ordinary men and women or forest spirits. He refrained from accompanying his drawings with narratives or engaging in any detailed oral explication, so it may be assumed either that these images have the

157–8

190

loose and allusive relationships to myth widely attested to in traditional art forms, or that they constitute a more personal corpus.

Mathias Kauage started work slightly after Akis and has produced many drawings, screenprints, copper panels and paintings; these are unlike Akis's in the sense that they display a fascination with new modes of transport, such as trucks and helicopters, and are replete with flags and references to national institutions. The distinctive treatment of passengers within these vehicles appears to draw upon the treatment of the face in Papuan and Sepik masks, although those traditions had no affinities with art in Kauage's home area of the north-eastern Highlands. The very freedom and energy of Kauage's work, together with that of Akis and a number of other artists who also come from the eastern Highlands, may stem paradoxically from the fact that the Highlands art forms – self-decoration, ephemeral plant installations around ritual sites, and architecture – could not be readily transposed

159–6

159 Mathias Kauage, *Okuk's son at Port Moresby airport*, 1987. 63⅞ × 72 in.

160 Mathias Kauage, *Man draiwim tripela member bilong hilans* (man driving the Highlands members of parliament), *c.* 1979. 18½ × 25¼ in.

to art for tourists or urban art. While neo-traditional artists from other regions were prompted to reproduce or adapt their traditional forms of carving and pottery, these individuals from the Highlands had to innovate in new media and have done so successfully.

159   Kauage's most effective works include a series concerning the Deputy Prime Minister, Iambakey Okuk, who died in 1987. These large paintings commemorated Okuk's accomplishments and depicted

162 Joe Nalo, *Legend of Leip Island*, 1993. 59 × 78¾ in.

scenes around his funeral (his son's return from the United States, for example) with much naive vigour. While the paintings in effect narrate a chapter in national political history, they were motivated by the fact that Okuk was a fellow clansman of Kauage's and much renowned among his own people, and the mood is accordingly one of assertive celebration rather than of mourning. While Kauage is interested in representations of the nation or modernity, such as flags and planes, these are used to emphasize the fame of this particular 'big-man'. Despite interest in novel institutions, modes of transport and art techniques, the values of the painting therefore seem entirely grounded in Highlands political culture (although Kauage's vision certainly also extends to national events, such as the Bougainville war).

The emerging Melanesian national cultures do not of course fully represent the varying groups and regions that actually constitute these nations: some regions have a higher political or cultural profile than others, and women are plainly marginalized. There has been much argument about gender relations in traditional and rural Papua New

193

161 (*opposite*) Mathias Kauage, *Buka War*, 1990. 49 × 68 in.

163 David Lasisi, *My Name*, 1987. 23⅜ × 24⅝ in.

164 David Lasisi, *The Deteriorated Image*, 1978. 25¼ × 24⅞ in.

Guinea, and the old missionary stereotype of primitive patriarchy needs to be substantially qualified, if not rejected, for most areas. As was shown in Chapter 5, apparent inequality often involved complementarity, and the ways in which women were and are valued, both by themselves and by men, have been neglected. However, the relaxation of sexual taboos and segregated space that followed conversion to Christianity eroded pre-existing spheres of female autonomy and restraints upon violence; much of the labour associated with novel forms of cash-cropping has fallen upon women; and alcohol has led to an increase in violence both in villages and in town. The picture is far more positive in areas other than the Highlands, but even if the pattern of broader social changes has been varied, it is difficult to avoid the view that the new nation state is no less a masculine instrument than the spearhead that provides the form for the Parliament House. The overwhelming male domination of government and bureaucracy has curiously also been manifest in the individualized, non-traditional art scene: in 1990 there were some fifteen prominent male painters and sculptors, but women who had been active earlier, in the late 1960s and early 1970s, appeared to have ceased work.

Women are, moreover, represented censoriously by Kauage and some other artists. In town and particularly at university, they are out of place and end up getting drunk, pregnant and selling themselves.

The traditional Highlands woman, who works hard and carries a full bilum, is idealized on the Parliament House facade and elsewhere, but the modern urban woman is garishly made up to entice expatriate men. Although this unambiguously negative projection might be taken as a distinctively Highlands attitude, it is present also in work representing urban prostitutes by other artists such as David Lasisi from New Ireland. All that is negative in the process of cultural change is projected onto women, while men who have entered new arenas such as national politics are only 'big-men' acting on a larger stage.

It should be stressed that while this is a prominent theme, not all artists approach women in this way, and women are emerging in other genres of non-traditional art. Wendy Choulai, for instance, is a fabric 166 designer who works primarily from Australia. Choulai has noted that the exclusion of women from traditional art, together with the tribal ownership of motifs and styles, has precluded her from translating traditional designs onto fabric, and she respects 'tribal copyright' even though she is not working within Papua New Guinea. She has therefore drawn more directly from her own perceptions of the environment and the power of ceremony and dance, and been broadly inspired by Asian, African and other Pacific art traditions. In Port Moresby, a number of women are working in pottery, one of the most accomplished being Mary Gole, whose work has both a local market 165 and wider exposure through such events as the Pacific Festivals of

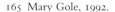

165 Mary Gole, 1992.

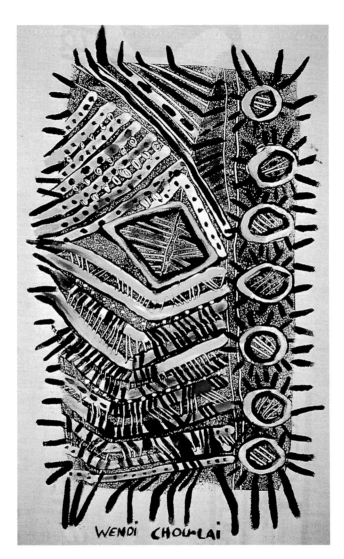

WENDi CHOULAI

166 Wendy Choulai, monoprint design for textile, 1987. 12 × 8 in.

167 (*opposite*) Emily Karaka, *Tangata Kore*, 1984. 62½ × 35¼ in.

the Arts, which occur roughly every four years. Although she grew up in a potting community in the Popendetta area in the north-east, Gole became a potter herself only later in life, in town, and has been stimulated not merely by the styles of her own area, but the wider range described and illustrated in Patricia May and Margaret Tuckson's book, *The Traditional Pottery of Papua New Guinea* (1982). This typifies the way in which outsiders' scholarly documentation can feed back

into local practice; here it enables work that synthesizes local traditions for new audiences and markets. Gole's pottery is not politically expressive in the fashion of official architecture, but it is just as much a reflection of a new national context in which cultural improvisation is flourishing.

The range of new Pacific art in New Zealand is similarly exciting, but Maori occupy a very different location in the postcolonial world

168 Selwyn Muru, *Tuupuna o te Whenua*, 1990. 22⅜ × 29⅞ in.

169 Michel Tuffery, poster for New Zealand International Festival of the Arts, 1994.

to the people of Papua New Guinea. From a pessimistic perspective, it could be argued that there is nothing postcolonial about their situation: the country is still occupied by the descendants of white settlers and other migrants, and Maori remain disadvantaged in multiple senses. Colonial relationships certainly endure, but they are in the process of being criticized, reflected upon and undone; and if this continues to be an incomplete process, it nevertheless entails deliberate efforts of decolonization and redefinition, which are particularly conspicuous in the domain of art.

198

Unlike Papua New Guinean artists, many Maori have been trained in art schools or combined 'Western' education with learning from their elders. They have used techniques, media and concepts like those employed in contemporary art elsewhere, to describe colonial relationships from a Maori perspective, to protest the violence of racism, to commemorate ancestors, past leaders and moments in political history and to draw attention to the power of traditional culture, while creating new modes of expression appropriate to the present. The most conspicuous problem in Papua New Guinea – that of imaging a national identity – is not a problem for Maori because the relationship of colonization constantly juxtaposes Maori and settler interests, creating a larger binary difference that overshadows the particular regional, historical and political differences separating Maori. Distinct tribal identities, and many other generational and biographical differences, however, remain important and many artists consciously address the false unity that a label such as 'Maori art' can impose.

Among the most senior artists is Paratene Matchitt, who began work in the 1950s. His most powerful works emerge from an interest since the early 1980s in the nineteenth- and early twentieth-century

171 (*above*) Brett Graham, *Lapita*, 1993. 45¼ × 31½ in. Without referring to the form or decoration of Lapita pottery, Brett Graham uses the substance and simplicity of a bowl to allude to the enduring significance of the Polynesian peoples' common ancestry. In other works he foregrounds the similar colonial experiences of Maori, Hawaiians and native north Americans.

170 (*left*) Kura Te Waru-Rewiri, *Whakapapa*, 1989. 3⅞ × 3⅞ in.

172 John Pule, *Style with Seven Moons*, 1993. 83½ × 71⅜ in.

Maori prophets, especially Te Kooti and Rua Kenana. It is not surprising that these figures should be of particular interest to a number of contemporary artists: in their time they sought to reform and transform Maori lifestyle in new communities, appropriating elements of Christianity and European power and adopting certain forms of European modernity. Architecture in the new communities often incorporated hybrid iconographies, which in Rua's case drew particularly upon hearts, spades, clubs and diamonds. It has been suggested that these playing-card motifs were used as mnemonic devices in Bible-study classes in the nineteenth century by converts unable to read and were perhaps taken as keys to secret forms of knowledge. Rua also used triangles, which stood for peace and the sacred mountain of Maungapohatu, where he had his visions; but they could also be inverted to resemble a sergeant's stripes and thus signify war.

Contemporary artists aim similarly to produce and re-evaluate symbols appropriate to evolving political relationships. In huge timber

173 (*opposite*) Paratene Matchitt, *Civic Square*, 1993.

and corrugated iron works, Matchitt not only pays homage to Rua's and Te Kooti's flags and icons, but by re-creating them in monumental form, he also affirms the power that the history still possesses. His 1993 work, dominating Civic Square (a pedestrian precinct in the nation's capital city), has a whole array of elements – birds, a whale and the ribs of a ship – that suggest movement and arrival, natural life and artifice. These, however, are overshadowed by poles bearing hearts and stars that stand out against Wellington's often turbulent and moody skies. The birds and whale do not necessarily represent an environment that might be appreciated or despoiled, but a contrast between the environment and the arrival of Europeans. However, the viewer is haunted more by the mysterious potential of a strand of Maori history that is still to run its course.   173

Emily Karaka's painting is marked by extreme pain and anger. Colonial violence and suffering are conveyed directly through tortuously dense oil paint evoking solidified tears and blood, a transcription of personal anguish over the loss of Maori land and life and the savagery of racism. In one powerful work, something like a traditional sculpture is shown to be decapitated; another images a tortured figure of Christ in association with several colonial treaties. The convoluted energies of Karaka's oil paintings frequently extend over the entire board or canvas, leaving no breathing space or border around the   167

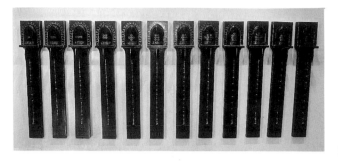

174 Robert Jahnke,
Conversion 3.33R, 1994.
9 ft 9⅜ in. × 48 in. × 8⅝ in.

edges. The burden of conflict would seem pervasive and oppressive, although other works by the artist have escaped this condition, imaging mountains, feet, words and motion in equally energetic compositions that suggest that icons and actions provide ground for transformation as well as sites of struggle.

174   Many other artists are concerned with the loss of land and power. Robert Jahnke has produced a series of assemblages in which axes are prominent: these were often exchanged for land by settlers and missions, and one emphasizes the 'conversion', not of pagans into Christians, but of forty thousand acres into twelve axes – a number of transactions of this kind were made by the Church Missionary Society. In one sense, such purchases seem a typically colonialist act of theft, in which objects of negligible value are substituted for a precious resource, but in Jahnke's treatment, the axe becomes almost as powerful as it must have appeared at the time to Maori, for whom rare iron tools had particular value. Like Rua's clubs and spades, the axe acquires a new significance that the Europeans who produced and introduced the motifs and objects could not have anticipated and do not control. The blade projecting outward from the assemblage threatens the viewer, reproducing the shocking inequality of the transaction, but rendering it ambiguous – we might know what the axe was, but we do not know what it has become. The sense of historical burden is reinforced literally and iconically: these are real axes wrapped in lead, a dull but heavy metal with lethal associations.

175–6   Robyn Kahukiwa, for some years concerned primarily with affirming the elemental power of Maori mythology and the particular importance of female deities, birth and genealogy, has turned more recently to a critical juxtaposition of contemporary women and those imaged in colonial studio photographs. Although these do not suggest some harmonious reintegration of colonial images into contemporary genealogies – the contemporary women appear disconcerted and alarmed rather than seeming examples of a new independence – these

202

175 Robyn Kahukiwa, *He Toa Takitahi*, 1985. 80¾ × 53¼ in.

176 (*below*) Robyn Kahukiwa, exhibition view of *White-Out*, 1994. Kahukiwa's work appeared alongside that of an Australian Aboriginal artist, Leah King-Smith, who was similarly interested in re-using nineteenth-century portraits and images in a critical way.

paintings reclaim a visual heritage and insist on its relationship to the identities of living Maori women.

While many artists concerned to evoke the space of meeting-houses and the presences of ancestors have imitated traditional carving, recent work has been increasingly adventurous and arguably more effective. Jacqueline Fraser's rhythmic, allusive figures and architectural environments, composed mainly of synthetic fibres, play across many boundaries, between Maori and Pakeha traditions, masculine and feminine,

177

decorative and structural. These works produce environments that are moving and that are no more readily translated into discourse than, say, the polysemous paintings of Sepik meeting-houses. They refuse any subordination to a traditionalist aesthetic, but are nevertheless irreducibly connected not only with the forms of traditional art, but also with its logic, for what is affirmed is, above all, presence: they are beautiful and gentle but also insistent. What they insist upon is the effect of a kind of Maori culture that is not rigidly traditionalist but enriched and extended by cultural exchange, and this insistence is the more effective for its expression in light, open and accessible forms. The audience in Aotearoa, if not elsewhere, may be surprised not by the work, but by the way they succumb to it, or the way it suggests a different self-knowledge. To put this in terms that recall my earlier discussion of Sepik Tambaran houses, these distinctly bicultural art forms may enable a collectivity to recognize its own sociality in novel postcolonial or dual cultural terms.

As Maori are differently situated from Papua New Guineans, migrant Polynesians – who form large communities in the United States and Australia, as well as in New Zealand – occupy a different location again within the postcolonial cultural order. They cannot claim the indigenous status that is so central to Maori affirmations, but they are concerned to use art to negotiate relations between old and new homes, to celebrate tradition and to create new forms of Polynesian culture that are meaningful for young second-generation migrants as well as those brought up in the islands. Fatu Feu'u, of Samoan background, is one of the most prominent figures; although he is primarily a painter, his elaborations of traditional motifs have been widely disseminated through screenprints and reproductions on postcards, shirts, carpets and ceramics. Although other Polynesian artists have questioned this degree of commercialization, it has given

178

177 Jacqueline Fraser, *He Tohu*, 31 July 1993–25 November 1993. Installation project, City Gallery, Wellington, New Zealand.

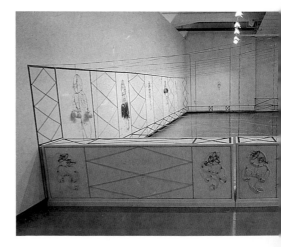

178 Fatu Feu'u, *After the Rain*, 1993.
65¾ × 56¼ in.

consumer culture in New Zealand a distinctive Pacific accent that is less politicized than the Maori cultural renaissance, but nevertheless a source of ethnic recognition and affirmation.

John Pule's paintings draw upon the compositional structure of neo-traditional Niuean barkcloth, but explore a more personal iconography. Canoe forms, which are also employed by other Pacific artists, refer to the process of settlement and to kin groups, but are incorporated into a kind of cartography: the paintings chart out his 172

home village and the tracts of land upon which his ancestors are buried; they also depict ships and movement away from Niue to New Zealand. But their energy emerges especially from the interaction between predatory, sexualized and transgressive figures such as sharks, birds and monsters; these are mythological creatures that in one sense have been left behind by those who have converted to Christianity, and those who have left the island for New Zealand, but that nevertheless continue to struggle, consume and animate one another.

While some Polynesian and Maori artists aim to express the cultural values of their communities in the broadest way, Pule is critical of the Christianity that most islanders continue to embrace. He sees the missionary intervention as a destructive one, bringing sorrow and sickness in much the same way as the nuclear testing in Micronesia and French Polynesia. He emphasizes the autocratic character of evangelists, who proscribed traditional sexual practices and insisted on the missionary position, while seeking to create new life in a religion that was dying in its European home: these concerns charge his paintings with erotic imagery, conflict and ambiguous crucifixions. There is a kind of allegory between the cultural loss that has been experienced in the Pacific, as a result of conversion, and the loss that migrants have sustained; but these paintings are not at all pessimistic. Pule, like a number of other new Pacific artists, uses his work to generate positive energy, to put art into the world in a way that can help cure individual ills and the wider problems of migrants who lack a sense of place. Despite its personal character, this art is part of a wider effort of collective affirmation.

179 Jim Vivieaere, *6 Tahitians, 2 in Leningrad, 4 in Papeete*, 1990. 16 × 11¼ in.

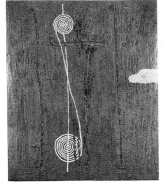

180 Peter Robinson, *Painting 1993*, 1993. 71¼ × 59⅞, 72 × 59⅞ in.

Some artists of both Polynesian migrant and Maori backgrounds find the wide interest in traditional motifs constrictive. Jim Vivieaere produces collages which sometimes draw upon barkcloth patterns but take equal interest in architectural forms seen in the course of European travel, as well as motifs from elsewhere: these are taken as available sources of inspiration, but not as a form of cultural property with which any artist has a privileged or unique connection. Other works by Vivieaere provide critical but amusing comment upon colonial representations of Polynesians: *6 Tahitians, 2 in Leningrad, 4 in Papeete* incorporates a cheap reproduction of a Gauguin painting   179 and a colonial postcard. The work draws attention to voyeurism and the absurd distance between real Tahitians and the location of the painting in a Russian museum, but also expresses potential for Polynesian reappropriation by affixing these images to the unmistakably indigenous surface of woven pandanus. This resistance to ethnic identifications is made more brutally explicit in paintings by Peter   180 Robinson, which question the artist's labelling as a Maori artist and the society's need to categorize artists in these terms: what they depict, writ large in oil on tar, is the number 3.125 – Robinson's own percentage of Maori blood.

In many parts of the Pacific, stylistic variation encoded and projected local cultural differences. Distinct art traditions made people's collectivity visible to themselves and to others. Art also voiced political views, negotiated male and female attributes, told stories, conveyed sacredness, armoured the person, marked secrecy and even worked violence. In the late twentieth century, Pacific art forms still do most of these things, but often in muted or implicit ways that we can discover and be surprised by. More visibly, art has come to serve projects of ethnic affirmation and cultural diplomacy.

Art is increasingly a domain through which people present their culture and heritage; once it is visible, they effectively become actors in a theatre of politics and in a multicultural marketplace. These uses of art do not distort the original meanings of culture, but represent pragmatic efforts that are related to some but not all the uses of art in precolonial situations.

Artists have worked both with and against this language of ethnic expression and cultural identity. They have articulated indigenous perspectives upon colonial history and indeed redefined both that history and the possible futures that follow from it. They have, however, also turned away from ethnic categorization and from the misleading unity that projects of cultuzral diplomacy tend to impose. Work by a Samoan artist tends to be read as an expression of Samoan culture, but it may equally address the artist's biography, and the common predicaments of people who live in a certain place, some of whom may be Samoan, Maori or white. These artists working in Western media may make collective statements, but, like the architects of Sepik Tambaran houses, they also allude to the provisional and artificial character of collectivity. Like many other conditions that Pacific art forms have evoked, ethnic identity is not a mystification, but the accomplishment of a moment; as one condition is expressed, others are masked or eclipsed. To describe a work of art as a work of Maori art or Polynesian art tells us something, but not everything; and it suppresses much of the diversity that continues to energize cultural creativity in the Pacific.

181 Michael Parekowhai, *Acts*, 1993. 78¾ × 78¾ in. This is an elaborated version of the children's game, Jack Straws. The objects resonate ambiguously with New Zealand's colonial history: the rifle, axe and saw suggest wars over land and the clearing of forests, while the ladder and crutch suggest the possibility of mutual aid.

Acknowledgments

For comments and practical assistance, I am grateful to Lissant Bolton, Rod Ewins, Niel Gunson, Steven Hooper, Christian Kaufman, Pat Kirch, Diane Losche, Roger Neich, Karen Nero, Michael O'Hanlon, Roger Rose, Markus Schindlbeck, Nikos Stangos, Hugh Stevenson and Don Tuzin. The suggestions and encouragement of Howard Morphy and Debbora Battaglia were especially valuable. I must thank particularly Maureen MacKenzie, whose material and inter-pretations form the basis of Chapter 5, and whose fine photographs I have used; and similarly Alfred Gell for the arguments about tattooing I have drawn upon in Chapter 4, and for many stimulating discussions about art, anthropology and the Pacific. My debt to Margaret Jolly arises from much more than the many suggestions she made about this book, which is for Anna; I hope that it and other projects have not taken away too much.

My sense of the dynamism of Pacific art owes a great deal to contact with artists and communities in the Marquesas, Fiji and Aotearoa (New Zealand). I owe more than I can say to those who have taken the time to discuss their own work, and in some cases their teaching and curatorial efforts. Most of these people cannot be named here, but I must thank Brett Graham, Robert Jahnke, Rangihiroa Panoho, Michael Parekowhai, John Pule and Jim Vivieaere.

Bibliography

General: Battaglia, D., 'Projecting Personhood in Melanesia: the dialectics of artefact symbolism on Sabarl Island', *Man*, 18, 1983, pp. 289–304. Brake, B., J. McNeish and D. Simmons, *Art of the Pacific*, Abrams, New York, 1980. Crawford, A. L., *Aida: Life and ceremony of the Gogodala*, Robert Brown/Cultural Council of Papua New Guinea, Bathurst, 1980. Forge, A. (ed.) *Art and Primitive Society*, Oxford University Press, New York, 1973. Ewins, R., *Fijian Artefacts*, Tasmanian Museum and Art Gallery, Hobart, 1982. Feldman, J. and D. Rubinstein, *The Art of Micronesia*, University of Hawaii Art Gallery, Honolulu, 1986. Gathercole, P., A. Kaeppler and D. Newton, *The Art of the Pacific Islands*, National Gallery of Art, Washington, 1979. Greub, S. (ed.), *Art of Northwest New Guinea*, Rizzoli, New York, 1992. Guiart, J., *The Arts of the South Pacific*, Thames and Hudson, London, 1963. Hanson, L. and F., *The Art of Oceania: a Bibliography*, G. K. Hall, Boston, 1984. Kaeppler, A., 'Artificial Curiosities': an exposition of native manufactures collected on the three Pacific voyages of Captain James Cook, R. N.*, Bishop Museum, Honolulu, 1978. Kirch, P., *The Evolution of the Polynesian Chiefdoms*, Cambridge University Press, Cambridge, 1984. May, P. and M. Tuckson, *The Traditional Pottery of Papua New Guinea*, Bay Books, Sydney, 1982. Mead, S. (ed.), *Exploring the Visual Art of Oceania*, University of Hawaii Press, Honolulu, 1979. Munn, N., 'The Spatiotemporal Transformations of Gawa Canoes', *Journal de la Société des Océanistes*, vol. 33, 1977, pp. 39–52. Nero, K. (ed.), *The Arts and Politics*, Pacific Studies (special issue), vol. 15, no. 4, 1992. Newton, D., C. Kaufman and A. Kaeppler, *L'art océanien*, Citadelles and Mazenod, Paris, 1993. O'Hanlon, M., *Reading the Skin: Adornment, Display and Society among the Waghi*, British Museum Press, London, 1989. O'Hanlon, M., *Paradise: Portraying the New Guinea Highlands*, British Museum Press, London, 1993. Phelps, S., *Art and Artifacts of the Pacific, Africa and the Americas*, Hutchinson, London, 1976. Sahlins, M., *Islands of History*, University of Chicago Press, Chicago, 1985. Schmitz, C., *Oceanic Art: Myth, Man and Image in the South Seas*, Abrams, New York, 1971. Smith, B., *European Vision and the South Pacific*, Yale University Press, New Haven, 1985. Speiser, F., *Ethnology of Vanuatu: an Early Twentieth Century Study*, Crawford House, Bathurst, 1990. Steinen, Karl von den, *Die Marquesaner und ihrer kunst*, Hacker Art Books, New York, 1925–8, reprinted 1969. Strathern, A. and M., *Self-decoration in Mount Hagen*, Duckworth, London, 1972. Strathern, M., *The Gender of the Gift*, University of California Press, Berkeley, 1988. Thomas, N., *Entangled Objects*, Harvard University Press, Cambridge, Mass., 1991. Weiner, A., *Inalienable Possessions*, University of California Press, Berkeley, 1992.

Chapter 1: Bowden, R., *Yena: Art and Ceremony in a Sepik Society*, Pitt Rivers Museum, Oxford, 1983. Forge, A., 'Art and Environment in the Sepik', *Proceedings of the Royal Anthropological Institute for 1965*, 1966, pp. 23–31. Forge, A., 'Style and Meaning in Sepik Art', in A. Forge (ed.), *Primitive Art and Society*, Oxford University Press, New York, 1973. Gell, A., *Metamorphosis of the Cassowaries*, Athlone Press, London, 1975. Losche, D., 'Male and Female in Abelam Society' (PhD dissertation, Columbia University), 1982. Newton, D., *Crocodile and Cassowary: Religious Art of the Upper Sepik River, New Guinea*, The Museum of Primitive Art, New York, 1971. Tuzin, D., *The Voice of the Tambaran: Truth and Illusion in Ilahita Arapesh Religion*, University of California Press, Berkeley, 1980.

Chapter 2: Hamilton, A., *Some Aspects of the Art Workmanship of the New Zealand Maori People* (also known as *Maori Art*), New Zealand Institute, Dunedin, 1896. Hanson, A., 'Art and the Maori Construction of Reality', in S. Mead and B. Kernot (eds), *Art and Artists in Oceania*, Dunmore Press, Palmerston North, New Zealand, 1983. Jackson, M., 'Aspects of Symbolism and Composition in Maori

Art, *Bijdragen tot de Taal-, Land- en Volkenkunde*, vol. 128, 1972, pp. 33–80. Neich, R., *Painted Histories: Early Maori Figurative Painting*, Auckland University Press, Auckland, 1993.

Chapter 3: Gerbrands, A., *Wowipits: Eight Asmat Wood-carvers of New Guinea*, Mouton, The Hague, 1967. Gerbrands, A. (ed.), *The Asmat of New Guinea: the Journal of Michael Rockefeller*, The Museum of Primitive Art, New York, 1967. Smidt, D. (ed.), *Asmat Art*, Braziller, New York, 1993. Waite, D., *Art of the Solomon Islands*, Musée Barbier-Müller, Geneva, 1983. Zegwaard, G., 'Jipae: Festival of the Mask Costumes', in D. Smidt (ed.), *Asmat Art*, Braziller, New York, 1993.

Chapter 4: Gell, A., *Wrapping in Images: Tattooing in Polynesia*, Oxford University Press, Oxford, 1993. Marquardt, C., *Die Tätowirung beider Geschlechter in Samoa*, Dietrich Reimer, Berlin, 1899. Oliver, D., *Ancient Tahitian Society*, University of Hawaii Press, Honolulu, 1974. Sulu'ape, Paulo II, 'Samoan Tattooing', in I. Wedde (ed.), *Fomison: What Shall We Tell Them?*, City Gallery, Wellington, 1994.

Chapter 5: Bolton, L., 'Dancing in Mats' (PhD thesis, University of Manchester), 1993. Jolly, M., 'Soaring Hawks and Grounded Persons: the politics of rank and gender in north Vanuatu', in M. Godelier and M. Strathern (eds), *Big Men and Great Men: Personifications of Power in Melanesia*, Cambridge University Press, Cambridge, 1991. Keller, J., Woven

World: Neotraditional Symbols of Unity in Vanuatu, *Mankind*, vol. 18, pp. 1–13. MacKenzie, M., *Androgynous Objects*, Harwood Academic Publishers, Chur, 1992. Weiner, A., *Women of Value, Men of Renown*, University of Texas Press, Austin, 1977.

Chapter 6: Hammond, J., *Tifaifai and Quilts of Polynesia*, University of Hawaii Press, Honolulu, 1986. Kooijman, S., *Tapa in Polynesia*, Bishop Museum, Honolulu, 1972. Robertson, H. A., *Erromanga: The Martyr Isle*, Hodder and Stoughton, London, 1903. Rutter, O. (ed.), *The Journal of James Morrison*, Golden Cockerel Press, London, 1935. Von Hügel, A., *The Fiji Journals of Baron Anatole von Hügel, 1875–1877*, J. Roth and S. Hooper (eds), Fiji Museum, Suva (1990).

Chapter 7: Gunson, N., 'Great Women and Friendship Contract Rites in Pre-Christian Tahiti', *Journal of the Polynesian Society*, vol. 73, 1964, pp. 209–53. Henry, T. *Ancient Tahiti*, Bishop Museum, Honolulu, 1928. Kaeppler, A., 'Hawaiian Art and Society: Traditions and Transformations', in A. Hooper and J. Huntsman (eds), *Transformations of Polynesian culture*, Polynesian Society, Auckland, 1985. Rose, R., *Symbols of Sovereignty: Feather Girdles of Tahiti and Hawaii*, Bishop Museum, Honolulu, 1980. Rose, R., *Hawaii: The Royal Isles*, Bishop Museum, Honolulu, 1980.

Chapter 8: Jernigan, E., 'Lochukle: A Palauan Art Tradition' (PhD dissertation, University of Arizona), 1973.

Keate, G., *An Account of the Pelew Islands*, London, 1790. Kramer, A., *Palau*, Friederichsen, Hamburg, 1917–29. Nero, K., 'The Breadfruit Tree Story: Mythological Transformations in Palauan Politics', in K. Nero (ed.), *The Arts and Politics, Pacific Studies* (special issue), vol. 15, 1992, pp. 235–60. Parmentier, R., *The Sacred Remains: Myth, History, and Polity on Belau*, University of Chicago Press, Chicago, 1987.

Chapter 9: Beier, G., *Modern Images from Niugini*, Jacaranda Press (special issue of *Kovave*), 1974. Hockin, J. P., *Supplement to the Account of the Panther and the Endeavour*, published as an appendix to G. Keate, *An Account of the Pelew Islands*, London, 1803. *Kohia ko taikaka anake: Artists Construct New Directions*, National Art Gallery, Wellington, 1993. Panoho, R., *Te Moemoea no Iotefa. The Dream of Joseph. A Celebration of Pacific Art and Taonga*, Serjeant Gallery, Wanganui, New Zealand, 1991. Rosi, P., 'Papua New Guinea's New Parliament House: A Contested National Symbol', *The Contemporary Pacific*, vol. 3, 1991, pp. 289–324. Simons, S. and H. Stevenson, *Luk luk gen! Look again! Contemporary Art from Papua New Guinea*, Perce Tucker Regional Gallery, Townsville, Queensland, 1991. Tamati-Quennell, M., *Pu Manawa* (on contemporary Maori weaving and related arts), National Museum, Wellington, 1993. Thomas, N., 'A Second Reflection: Presence and Opposition in Maori Art', *Journal of the Royal Anthropological Institute*, 1995.

List of illustrations

representing wood spirit, Palimbai, Iatmul, East Sepik, *c.* 1931–2. Cambridge University Museum of Archaeology and Anthropology. Photo Gregory Bateson.

49 Hoisting ridgepole of ceremonial house in East Sepik, Papua New Guinea, 1971. Photo Donald Tuzin.

50 Facade painting from Abelam house, central Sepik. Ht 64⅝ (164). Painted barkcloth. Museum für Völkerkunde, Basel.

51 Bowl, Marquesas Islands. Ht 5, Diam. 12 (12.7 × 30.5). Wood. Museum für Völkerkunde, Basel.

52 Carved and painted house, Wairarapa. The Museum of New Zealand (*Te Papa Tongarewa*), Wellington, New Zealand. B9794.

53 *Pou tokomanawa*, Mamaku, Hicks Bay, collected 1910. Ht 54⅜ (138). Wood. Otago Museum, Dunedin. Photo Lindsay McLeod.

54 *Poupou* in style of the Te Arawa. Wood. Present location unknown. Photo The Museum of New Zealand (*Te Papa Tongarewa*), Wellington, New Zealand. B15248.

55 *Pataka*, Lake Taupo, 1878. 6⅞ × 10¾ (17.3 × 27.3). Wanganui Regional Museum, New Zealand.

56 Meeting-house of Hotunui. Wood and weaved matting. Auckland Institute and Museum, Auckland.

57 Barge board support from a Te Awhi *pataka*. Ht 29⅛ (74). Wood. The Museum of New Zealand (*Te Papa Tongarewa*), Wellington, New Zealand. B18965.

58 Canoe stern-piece, *taurapa*, collected *c.* 1826–9. Ht 54 (137). Painted wood. Musée national des Arts d'Afrique et d'Océanie, Paris. Photo Dominique Genet.

59 *Pare*. 14⅜ × 42½ (36.4 × 108). Wood. The Museum of New Zealand (*Te Papa Tongarewa*), Wellington, New Zealand. B18726.

60 *Kowhaiwhai* painting from the Manutuke church, constructed 1849–63. Ht 58⅝ (149). Painted wood. The Museum of New Zealand (*Te Papa Tongarewa*), Wellington, New Zealand. B17784.

61 Detail of a club, Marquesas Islands. Ht 54 (137). Wood. Private collection. Photo Hugues Dubois/Musée Dapper, Paris.

62 Door frame, Ngati Whatua tribe, Otakanini, 1500–1800. Ht 8 ft ½ (245). Wood. Auckland Institute and Museum, Auckland. Photo Krzysztof Pfeiffer.

63 Dendroglyph, Hapupu, east coast, Chatham Islands. Photo courtesy Michael King.

64 Tene Waitere at work. Alexander Turnbull Library, Wellington. G70071 1/1.

65 Carving of the deity Maui by Tene Waitere, 1898–9. Ht 7 ft ⅝ (215). Wood. Hamburgisches Museum für Völkerkunde, Hamburg.

66 *Hei-tiki*, 1500–1800. Ht 4¾ (12). Nephrite, fibre and bone. Musée national des Arts d'Afrique et d'Océanie, Paris.

67 Feather cape, made by Makurata Paitini, Tuhoe tribe, *c.* 1900. 41⅜ × 53½ (105 × 136). Kahukura feathers and fibre. Auckland Institute and Museum, Auckland.

68 *Bisj* poles, Buepis village, Fajit River, Casuarina Coast, south-west New Guinea. Photo Tobias Schneebaum.

69 Mask costumes of *jipae* festival, Amanamkai village, central Asmat, 1961. Photo Adrian A Gerbrands.

70 Shield, Unir River, north-west Asmat, collected 1913. Ht 75⅝ (192). Wood, lime, red ochre and charcoal. Rijksmuseum voor Volkenkunde, Leiden. Photo Isaäc C. Brussee.

71 Shield, made by Tjokotsj, Atjametsj village, central Asmat, collected 1961. Wood, lime, red ochre, charcoal, sago leaf, fibre and Abrus seeds. 65¾ (167). Rijksmuseum voor Volkenkunde, Leiden. Photo Ben Grishaaver.

72 Shield, carved by Ndaji, Manep village, upper Unir River and Utumbuwe River area, north-west Asmat, collected 1970. 71⅝ (182). Wood, lime, red ochre and charcoal. Rijksmuseum voor Volkenkunde, Leiden. Photo Ben Grishaaver.

73 Shield, Woméni village, Suwa River, Citak, collected *c.* 1954. 75⅜ (191.5). Wood, chalk, red ochre and charcoal. Rijksmuseum voor Volkenkunde, Leiden. Photo Ben Grishaaver.

74 Asmat motifs.

75 War Chief of Owa Raha, Eastern Solomon Islands, *c.* 1930. From Hugo Bernatzik, *Travels in the South Seas*, London, 1935.

76 *Kapkap*, Solomon Islands. W. 5 (12.8) Tridacna-shell and tortoise shell. Private collection, New York.

77 Exhibition view of Solomon Island canoes, Übersee Museum, Bremen, 1993. Photo Nicholas Thomas.

78 Inlaid bowl, Solomon Islands, collected nineteenth century. L. 25 (64.5). Wood and shell. © The Field Museum, Chicago, Il. A97422.

79 Canoe figurehead (*Nguzunguzu*), Marovo Lagoon, New George, Solomon Islands, collected 1929. Ht 6¾ (17). Painted wood. Museum für Völkerkunde, Basel.

80 Shield with inlay, Solomon Islands. Ht 31⅛ (79). Wood and pearl. © The Field Museum, Chicago, Il. A97067.

81 Lipped club, Fiji. Ht 24⅛ (61.3). Wood. Museum of Primitive Art, New York.

82 Club, Tonga. Ht 43¾ (111). Wood with ivory inlay. Collection of Mark and Carolyn Blackburn.

83 Detail of coconut-stalk club, Tonga, collected *c.* 1824. Ht 36 ¼ (92). © The Field Museum, Chicago, Il. A97367.

84 Tomika Te Mutu, nineteenth-century Maori chief. Photo John Hillelson Agency.

85 Nineteenth-century Samoan male tattoo. From Carl Marquardt, *Die Tätowirung beider Geschlecter in Samoa*, Berlin, 1899.

86 Tahitian tattoos, sketched by Sydney Parkinson, 1769. Pencil and wash. By permission of the British Library, London. Add MS 23921 folio 51 verso.

87 Paetini, chiefly woman of Taiohae, Nukuhiva, northern Marquesas Islands, 1838. From J. S. C. Dumont D'Urville, *Voyage au Pôle Sud*, 1841–7.

88 Portrait of New Zealand man with tattoos, by Sydney Parkinson, 1773. Pencil and wash. 15¼ × 11⅝ (38.7 × 29.5). By permission of the British Library.

89 Chief or chiefly attendant with tattoos, Sandwich Islands. From Louis Claude Desaulses de Freycinet, *Voyage autour du monde*, 1824–6.

90 Tattooing in Samoa, late nineteenth century. From Carl Marquardt, *Die Tätowirung beider Geschlecter in Samoa*, 1899.

91 Fully tattooed Marquesan man, engraving after a drawing made in 1804. From G. H. von Langsdorf, *Voyages and travels in various parts of the world*, London, 1813–14.

92 Male tattoo designs, Marquesas Islands. From Karl von den Steinen, *Die Marquesaner und ihrer Kunst*, Berlin, 1925–8.

93 Carved arm with tattoo designs, Marquesas Islands, collected by Robert Louis Stevenson, *c.* 1890–4, Ht 24 (61). Wood. Peabody and Essex Museum, Salem.

94 Anthropomorphic figure with two heads, Tahiti, Society Islands, collected 1822. Ht 23 (58.5). Wood. Trustees of the British Museum, London.

95 The beachcomber John Rutherford. From H. Ling Roth, 'Tatu in the Society Islands', *Journal of the Royal Anthropological Institute*, 35, 1905.

96 Samoan tattooing in Auckland, New Zealand, 1982. Photo Mark Bentley Adams.
97 Vicki Te Amo, 1993. Photo Margaret Kawharu.
98 Detail of weaving by Telefol women, 1983. Photo Maureen MacKenzie.
99 Woman collecting plant fibres, 1982. Photo Maureen MacKenzie.
100 Two women with bilums, 1982. Photo Maureen MacKenzie.
101 Man with feather bilum, 1981. Photo Maureen MacKenzie.
102 Young Baktaman man being painted for initiation ceremony, 1981. Photo Maureen MacKenzie.
103 Christian revivalist women, 1984. Photo Maureen MacKenzie.
104 Detail of mat, Pentecost Island, Vanuatu, collected 1912. 12 ft 11½ × 33½ (400 × 85). Museum für Völkerkunde, Basel.
105 Distribution of mats, Saraisese, East Ambae, 1992. Photo Lissant Bolton.
106 Papua New Guinea bilum, 1990. Photo Michael O'Hanlon.
107 Basket, West Futuna, Vanuatu. Base: L. 8¼, W. 6¼ (21, 16). Photo from the collection of Janet Dixon Keller. Photo Dave Minor.
108 Antoine Claude Francois Villerey, *Barkcloth making, House of Kraimokou, First Minister to the King, Sandwich Island, c.* 1819. 9¼ × 12⅝ (23.5 × 32). Engraving. National Library of Australia, Canberra.
109 Tapa anvil, Marquesas Islands, nineteenth century. 6¼ × 6½ × 30 (16 × 16.5 × 76.5). Wood. Linden-Museum, Stuttgart. Photo Ursula Didoni.
110 Page from Alexander Shaw, *Catalogue of the different specimens of cloth collected in the three voyages of Captain Cook to the southern hemisphere,* 1787. Mitchell Library, State Library of New South Wales, Australia.
111 Barkcloth, Erramanaga, southern Vanuatu, late nineteenth century. 76 × 31–34 (193 × 78.7–86.4). Photo John Fields, copyright Australian Museum, Sydney. Neg 1751m7.
112 Tapa from, top to bottom: Futuna, Tonga, Lau in Fiji and Hawaii. Courtesy National Museum of Natural History, Smithsonian Institution, Washington D.C.
113 Women of Nalimolevu clan, Ekubu Village, Vatulele Island, Fiji, July 1993. Photo Roderick Ewins.
114 Chief of Borabora, Society Islands, drawn by L. J. Duperrey in Louis Claude Desaulses de Freycinet, *Voyage autour du monde,* 1824–6.

115 John Webber, *Waheiadooa, Chief of Oheitepeha lying in state, c.* 1777–89. 16⅝ × 22¾ (42.2 × 57.8). Watercolour. Dixson Galleries, State Library of New South Wales, Australia.
116 Niuean barkcloth, nineteenth century. 78¾ × 51⅛ (200 × 130). The Museum of New Zealand (*Te Papa Tongarewa*), Wellington, New Zealand. F913/3.
117 Theodore Kleinschmidt, drawing of Tui Nadrau, October 1877. Hamburgisches Museum für Völkerkunde, Hamburg.
118 Tapa figure, Rapanui. Ht 16⅛ (41). Painted barkcloth on a wooden frame. Peabody Museum of Archaeology and Ethnology, Cambridge.
119 Barkcloth skirt, Futuna, late nineteenth or early twentieth century. 62¼ × 38⅝ (158 × 98). The Museum of New Zealand (*Te Papa Tongarewa*), Wellington, New Zealand. F913/4.
120 Costume mat, Marshall Islands, late nineteenth to early twentieth century. 35⅞ × 35 (91 × 89). The Museum of New Zealand (*Te Papa Tongarewa*), Wellington, New Zealand. B24606.
121 Barkcloth with patterns based on tattooing designs, Fatuiva, southern Marquesas Islands, *c.* 1984. 41⅜ × 35⅜ (105 × 90). Private collection, Canberra. Photo Instructional Resources Unit, Australian National University, Canberra.
122 *Ke kumum waina* (grapevine), Hawaii, before 1918. 7 ft × 7 ft (213.5 × 213.5). Appliqué quilt, white cotton with calico appliqué (turkey red), machine-stitched quilting (pattern in four units). Honolulu Academy of Arts, Hawaii. Gift of Mr and Mrs Richard A. Cooke, 1927.
123 Maria Teokolai and others, *Ina and the Shark, c.* 1990. 8 ft 5 × 8 ft 1⅛ (257 × 247). *Tivaevae* (ceremonial quilt). The Museum of New Zealand (*Te Papa Tongarewa*), Wellington, New Zealand. B24769.
124 Carved stool, Cook Islands, nineteenth century. 5 × 16⅛ × 8⅜ (12.6 × 41.2 × 21.3). Wood. The Robert and Lisa Sainsbury Collection, University of East Anglia, Norwich. Photo James Austin.
125 Fly whisk, Samoa. Ht 20 (50.8). Wood and fibre. Phoebe A. Hearst Museum of Anthropology, University of California at Berkeley.
126 Fly whisk, Tubuai, Austral Islands. Ht 35 (89). Wood, plant fibre, feathers and mother-of-pearl. Peabody Museum of Natural History, New Haven.
127 William Bligh, sketch of a Tahitian

feather girdle, 1792. 12⅜ × 7¾ (31.4 × 19.7). Watercolour. Mitchell Library, State Library of New South Wales, Australia.
128 Feather gods, Hawaii, collected 1778–9. Hts 24¾ and 40⅛ (63 × 102). Basket, feathers, hair, shell, mother-of-pearl and teeth. Trustees of the British Museum, London.
129 Feather *leis*. Ls 25, 24 and 23 (63.5 × 61 × 58.4). Feathers and ribbon. Bishop Museum, Honolulu.
130 Feather cape, Hawaii, collected 1778–9. L. 50¾ (129). Feathers and fibre. Copyright Australian Museum, Sydney.
131 *Kahili*. Feathers and ribbon. Bishop Museum, Honolulu.
132 Ku, God of War, Hawaii. Ht 78¾ (200). Wood. Trustees of the British Museum, London.
133 Ritual adze, Mangaia, Cook Islands, collected 1891. Ht 12⅞ (32.6). Stone blade, wooden handle and fine sennit. Museum of Anthropology and Ethnography, St Petersburg.
134 Decorated bottle gourd, Hawaii. Ht 8¼, Diam. 11 (21, 28). Bishop Museum, Honolulu. Photo Seth Joel.
135 Duck and chicken feather cape, made in England *c.* 1824. W. 28, L. 22½ (71, 57). Peacock, mallard duck, parrot, chicken and other feathers; linen and thread. Bishop Museum, Honolulu. Photo Seth Joel.
136 Detail of fine mat with feather fringe, Samoa. 60 × 60 (152.4 × 152.4). Pandanus and red feathers. Bishop Museum, Honolulu.
137 Figure of deity, A'a, Rurutu, Austral Islands, collected 1820. Ht 44 (111.7). Wood. Trustees of the British Museum, London.
138 Detail of engraved bamboo tube, New Caledonia. Territorial Museum, Nouméa, New Caledonia.
139 Loom-woven textile, attributed to Kosrae, Caroline Islands, nineteenth century. 9 ft 1½ × 8⅝ (278 × 22). The Museum of New Zealand (*Te Papa Tongarewa*), Wellington, New Zealand. B24742.
140 *Bai*, Airai, Belau, Caroline Islands.
141 Detail of money motif from *bai*, Belau, Caroline Islands. Collected 1909. Hamburgisches Museum für Völkerkunde, Hamburg. Photo Nicholas Thomas.
142 Engraving after a 1790 sketch of *bai*, Belau, Caroline Islands. From G. Keate, *An Account of the Pelew Islands,* 1790.
143 *Bai* facade, Belau, *c.* 1908–10. From Augustin Kramer, *Palau,* 1929.

213

144 Figure of goddess Dilukai, from *bai* facade, Belau, Caroline Islands, collected by Augustin Kramer, *c.* 1908–10. Ht 25⅞ (65.6). Painted wood. The Metropolitan Museum of Art, New York. The Michael C. Rockefeller Memorial Collection.
145 *Bai* facade, Belau, *c.* 1908–10. From Augustin Kramer, *Palau*, 1929.
146 Storyboard depicting magical breadfruit tree, Belau. 8¼ × 23¾ (21 × 60.3). Painted wood. Bishop Museum, Honolulu. Photo Christine Takata.
147 Storyboard depicting tale of the dissatisfied wife, Belau. 6¾ × 25 (17.1 × 63.5). Painted wood. Bishop Museum, Honolulu. Photo Christine Takata.
148 Breadfruit tree billboard, 1983. Photo Karen L. Nero.
149 Storyboard, attributed to Simon Novep, Kambot village, Keram river, Sepik province. 39⅜ × 63 (100 × 160). Painted wood. Museum für Völkerkunde, Basel.
150 Detail of paddle, Buka, Papua New Guinea. Ht 67⅛ (170.5). Painted wood. The Metropolitan Museum of Art, New York. The Michael C. Rockefeller Memorial Collection.
151 Detail of paddle, Buka, Papua New Guinea, *c.* 1900. 50 × 4½ (127 × 11.5). Painted wood. Staatliche Museen zu Berlin – Preussischer Kulturbesitz Museum für Völkerkunde. Photo Dietrich Graf.
152 Tie-beam from custom or canoe house, Uki Island, eastern Solomon Islands, collected 1865. L. 15 ft ⅛ (461). From Julius L. Brenchley, *The Cruise of the Curaçoa*, London, 1873.
153 Martin Morububuna, *The Young Nation of Papua New Guinea*, *c.* 1978. 22 × 29½ (56 × 75). Screenprint 27/30. Flinders University Art Museum Collection, Adelaide.
154 Ruki Fame, *Man on Bicycle*, 1975. Ht 21⅝, W. 17¾ (55, 45). Welded metals. Photo Kate Lowe, copyright Australian Museum, Sydney.
155 Papua New Guinea Banking Corporation, Port Moresby. Designed by David Lasisi, 1976. Photo Hugh Stevenson.
156 Parliament House, Waigani, 1983. Photo Hugh Stevenson.
157 Timothy Akis, untitled drawing, *c.* 1977. 40⅛ × 25¼ (102 × 64). Ink on cartridge paper. Photo Kate Lowe, copyright Australian Museum, Sydney. Neg 7415m.
158 Timothy Akis, *Palau na munuk* (cassowary and lizard), *c.* 1979. 29⅛ × 20½ (74 × 52). Screenprint. Private collection, Canberra. Photo Instructional Resources Unit, Australian National University, Canberra.
159 Mathias Kauage, *The Life and Death of Iambakey Okuk*, 1987. 63⅞ × 72 (162.3 × 182.9). Acrylic on canvas. Photo Ric Bolzan, copyright Australian Museum, Sydney.
160 Mathias Kauage, *Man draiwim tripela member bilong hilans* (man driving the Highlands members of parliament), *c.* 1979. 18½ × 25¼ (47 × 64). Screenprint. Private collection, Canberra. Photo Instructional Resources Unit, Australian National University, Canberra.
161 Mathias Kauage, *Buka War*, 1990. 49 × 68 (124.5 × 172.7). Acrylic on canvas. Photo Eileen Tweedy.
162 Joe Nalo, *Legend of Leip Island*, 1993. 59 × 78¾ (150 × 200). Oil on canvas. Museum für Völkerkunde, Frankfurt. Photo Hugh Stevenson.
163 David Lasisi, *My Name*, 1987. 23⅜ × 24⅝ (59.4 × 62.2). Screenprint. Hugh Stevenson Collection, Sydney.
164 David Lasisi, *The Deteriorated Image*, 1978. 25¼ × 24⅞ (64 × 62.5). Screenprint 75/89. Flinders University Art Museum Collection, Adelaide.
165 Mary Gole, 1992. Photo David Gole.
166 Wendy Choulai, monoprint design for textile, 1987. 12 × 8 (30 × 20). Photo courtesy Jackie Lewis-Harris.
167 Emily Karaka, *Tangata Kore*, 1984. 62½ × 35¼ (158.8 × 89.4). Oil on hessian. Sarjeant Gallery, Wanganui.
168 Selwyn Muru, *Tuupuna o te Whenua*, 1990. 22⅜ × 29⅞ (56.7 × 76). Lithograph. The Museum of New Zealand (*Te Papa Tongarewa*), Wellington, New Zealand. B037201.
169 Michael Tuffery, *I'll see you at the dance tonite* (*Sau ta eva le siva nanei*), for poster for New Zealand International Festival of the Arts, 1994.
170 Kura Te Waru-Rewiri, *Whakapapa*, 1989. 3⅞ × 3⅜ (10 × 8.5). Lithograph. The Museum of New Zealand (*Te Papa Tongarewa*), Wellington, New Zealand. B037200.
171 Brett Graham, *Lapita*, 1993. 45¼ × 31½ (115 × 80). Hawkesbury stone. Private collection.
172 John Pule, *Style with Seven Moons*, 1993. 83½ × 71⅝ (212 × 182). Oil on canvas. Private collection, Canberra. Courtesy Judith Anderson Gallery, Auckland. Photo Mark Adams.
173 Paratene Matchitt, *Civic Square*, 1993. Photo Nicholas Thomas.
174 Robert Jahnke, *Conversion 3.33R*), 1994. 9 ft 9⅜ × 48 × 8⅞ (298 × 122.1 × 22.5). Lead, wood and solder. Courtesy Fox Gallery, Auckland.
175 Robyn Kahukiwa, *He Toa Takitahi*, 1985. 80¾ × 53¼ (205 × 135.2). Alkyd oil on canvas. Sarjeant Gallery, Wanganui.
176 Robyn Kahukiwa, exhibition view of *White-Out*, 1994. Photo Nicholas Thomas.
177 Jacqueline Fraser, *He Tohu*, 31 July 1993–25 November 1993. Installation project, City Gallery, Wellington, New Zealand.
178 Fatu Feu'u, *After the Rain*, 1993. 65¾ × 56¼ (167 × 143). Oil on canvas. Collection of the artist. Photo Michael Roth.
179 Jim Vivieaere, *6 Tahitians, 2 in Leningrad, 4 in Papeete*, 1990. 16 × 11¼ (40.5 × 28.5). Collage and colour xerox. Collection of Rangihiroa and Adrienne Panoho, Wellington.
180 Peter Robinson, *Painting 1993*, 1993. 71¼ × 59⅞, 72 × 59⅞ (181 × 152, 183 × 152). Oil, tar and wax on canvas. The Museum of New Zealand (*Te Papa Tongarewa*), Wellington, New Zealand. B36998.
181 Michael Parekowhai, *Acts*, 1993. 78¾ × 78¾ (200 × 200). Wood and enamel paint. Auckland City Art Gallery, Auckland. Photo Nicholas Thomas.

Index